How to go from
Frazzled
T o
Fantastic

A Step-by-Step Guide to
Manage Your Stress,
Stop Your Worry and
Feel Fantastic Every Day

By
Gia Cilento

MH MAD HATTER PUBLISHING INC.

For information or bulk purchases:
Mad Hatter Publishing, Inc.,
P.O. Box 20973
Ferndale, MI 48220.
MadHatterPublishingInc.com

Cover image by Miroslav Ambruš-Kiš hosted on Unsplash.com

Gia Cilento
How to Go From Frazzled to Fantastic – A Step-by-Step Guide to Manage
Your Stress, Stop Your Worry, and Feel Fantastic Every Day
ISBN: 978-0-9994692-0-0 (Paperback)

Notice: The information given here is designed to help you make
informed changes in your life. This book is not intended to take the place
of professional, medical, psychological or other treatment. If you're under
a doctor's care, please consult with them before using the procedures
outlined in this book. If any recommendations given in this book
contradict the treatment you're currently following, be sure to consult
them prior to proceeding.
Mention of specific products, companies, organizations, or authorities in
this book does not imply endorsement by the author or the publisher; nor
does mention of specific companies, organizations, or authorities imply
that they endorse this book.
The author and the publisher disclaim any liability or loss, personal or
otherwise, resulting from the procedures in this program.
The mention or reference to any products, courses, or trademarks is
intended to benefit the owner of such and is not intended to infringe upon
trademark, copyright, or other rights; nor to imply any claim to the mark
other than that made by the owner. No endorsement of the information
contained in this book has been given by the owners of such products and
trademarks, and no such endorsement is implied by the inclusion of
product pictures or trademarks in this book.

For Wendy, Naomi, Sean, Andrea, Micah, and Diana – you are my inspiration and reason for getting up in the morning. I love you with all my heart.

Thank you for ordering this MHPI book. Sign up to hear all about our authors, their latest books, and our upcoming Giveaways. Plus – get exclusive early access to all our launch events. Visit us online at:
MadHatterPublishingInc.com

Contents

☺
Foreword

You don't know me - yet. So, it's wise to start your journey through this book from a place of neutrality. Give yourself some time with the concepts in this book. Some of them you may have heard of, some you may not. Some may make sense and you'll want to incorporate them right away, some you may think stupid or scary or worthless.

That's great! That means your mind is working. You're using your critical decision-making skills in an effective and useful manner.

Ten years ago when the bottom fell out of the real estate market and the economy took a nosedive, my personal economy also took a dump, too. Coincidence? Who knows?

I lost everything. My home, my business, my lover, my best friend (to suicide) and even my dog. I hit rock bottom and walked away with the clothes on my back and whatever I could fit in my little car.

Puh-thetic, eh? Well, I felt pathetic. It was one of the lowest points I'd ever experienced. I blamed everyone, grew angry and then depressed.

But, I'm not finished yet. See, this wasn't the first time I'd lost everything. Almost 10 years earlier, I'd had a bad car accident that laid me flat on my back for 6 months and in therapy for more than two years.

I could barely walk, couldn't remember how to make a shopping list or balance a checkbook, couldn't understand anything I read, and couldn't stand up long enough to make dinner for my kids who were 15 and 16 at the time.

I'd been skyrocketing in the Fortune 100 Company where I worked and this brought my career to a screeching halt. You can't climb a ladder, let alone break through any glass ceilings when you're not there for half a year (more really, I couldn't work more than 12 hours a week for a couple more years ... it was rough).

Before that, there was the divorce in my mid-20's. I won't go into the grisly details but suffice to say – I lost it all then, too. So, when the recession struck, I was still on the climb back up from the car crash. I wasn't fully whole again, my brain was still healing, so it hit me hard and took me even lower emotionally.

I've spent the past 10 years healing and building my life up, once again. That may sound like a long time but it was what I could manage and it was worth it. I've never felt better in my life.

I've built myself up from the inside out. I knew, deep down, that most of the work I had to do was internal. I had to repair my self-esteem. Rebuild my confidence. Allow my brain to continue healing from the mild Traumatic Brain Injury, and find a way to repackage all my skills, talents and knowledge into something I could call a career.

I found out I couldn't go back to corporate life, though I tried. I'd been a business owner, consultant, and an independent contractor for too long after the accident and was no longer corporate material. Plus, I was in my late 40's and the recession had millions out of work. I was a statistic.

I ended up working in various part-time retail jobs over several years and waited it out. At the time, it felt like I had no future, as though I was worthless. I lost hope for a while, believing that, because I wasn't making enough money or working in the type of job I was accustomed to, I was washed up.

I knew I had to find a way to feel a sense of pride in myself again and put the joy back into my life. Actually, put joy into my life for perhaps the first time since I was a small child.

I remember the first time I actually realized that I felt good on the inside. I was sitting at home, having a cup of coffee. I'd finished my morning meditation, had been awake for a bit and it struck me, I felt good. I felt happy. I did an internal check and found that I didn't feel any anxiety anywhere. It usually showed up as tension in my neck and shoulders and a stomach ache, something I'd experienced since I was about 8-10 years old.

As I played out my morning, I realized that I'd woken up feeling this way. This was new and wonderful. Waking up free from that horrible, nagging feeling of impending doom (I know it sounds melodramatic but that's really how I woke up every morning of my life before this). I was FREE!

Now, after years of work, introspection, experimentation, thousands of dollars on course after course, method after method, I'd passed the tipping point. I created a new way of being and from there, everything flowed. I now have a successful business, a fantastic relationship, and a thriving, loving family.

So, this is the reason I'm writing this book. After dragging myself out of the pit I'd descended into, I want to share. I've always enjoyed volunteering and making a contribution and have been involved in one form or another most of my life. As a tutor in elementary school, caring for the new-born babies at Mount Sinai Hospital in Miami, participating in Habitat for Humanity builds, helping build a computer lab and music studio for the Boys and Girls Club, and providing food for needy families, I've always gained a sense of satisfaction by lending a hand to others.

Taking care of myself, however, is a newly discovered behavior. While I've gained mightily, I've come to realize even more powerfully, how important it is to share my Self and what I've learned, not because you can't get there on your own, if you want to, but because I've already blazed a path and I can shine some light on your path as you progress.

I'll show you how I made my way down that path of healing, fulfillment, and joy. I'll share what I've learned, the methods that made a huge difference and those that became a part of my everyday life, my everyday thinking and helped me re-form my inner landscape into a place where I feel confident, safe, loving, powerful and able to withstand whatever happens in the world. There is such a thing as Unconditional Joy and you'll find out about it here.

I hope you also find inspiration, a solid path – well lit, and tools and insights that will help you on your journey.

You are more powerful than you can imagine and sometimes you need to look outside yourself to realize it. Your path of self-discovery leads you to who you really are, what's more, it leads to the creation of a wide-open, fun-filled, fantastic life.

This book (and the course, too) steps you through how to take care of your Self, especially your inner world, how to identify and deal with your demons, realize that they're just smoke and mirrors, get a hold of your emotions and use them to your advantage, harness your energy, and use it to propel you into a phase of life that you've only dreamt of before.

I am SO excited to start this journey with you, to lead you and make new discoveries together. To be clear, I'm not saying that my journey is over, I know it's just begun. I'm saying I've reached a certain point and from here, I know I can reach out and help others who may not have clarity about which direction to take.

I'm here. I made it. I'm still alive and I know that you can come out of the depths of despair, anxiety, or whatever plagues you and still lead a joyful life, too. The biggest factor is you.

You have to make the choice. YOU have to have a lightbulb go off at some juncture and realize that there's a better way. There's an availability of fulfillment, confidence, self-esteem and full-out joy that is just waiting for you to turn your head slightly and go in a different direction.

☺
Introduction

So, you're here and you have this book, or at least part of it if you're looking at the sample, and you want to know if it's worth actually reading any further. Well, this is where I tell you all the good things you'll get in your life once you're finished reading.

Thing is, I don't really have an answer to that. I mean, really, how would I know what it is you truly want out of life or what joy looks like to you? I don't know you and you don't know me. You'll know a lot more about me once you get into this book and make your way through it, but I won't really know much more about you.

I won't know how committed you are to taking good care of yourself. I won't know your starting point or what catalyzed you into pursuing your journey. I won't know your pain and I won't know your torments. I won't know what makes you tick or what makes you feel.

Really, the only thing I'll know for certain is that you're on a journey, and that's what we have in common. You're on a journey and you're looking for signposts along the way to help you know that you're heading in the right direction.

That's what I did, after all. I looked for those who might be a bit further down the path, who took the time to share their story, their successes and failures, in hopes that they might shed a bit of light on my path as I walked along it (or stumbled as happens at times). I read everything that came my way, took courses, spent thousands upon thousands of dollars in my search for clarity and purpose and a sense of calm within my inner landscape.

It makes sense to me that you would look for a bit of light-shedding upon your path as well. It seems to me that it's not only an act of sharing but a responsibility to those who are searching, to throw my bits and pieces into the fray, too, and hope that someone will benefit. Hope that my words, in the order I write them, with the style and phrasing and silliness or what have you, hits the spot for someone who's searching. How deliriously wonderful would that be!

You may want to read this book through once and then pick out the exercises, meditations, journal topics, and other approaches you'd like to use. Conversely, you may want to browse the Table of Contents and pick and choose right away, not bothering with those parts that don't appeal or that you may already think you know or have used.

Whichever method you choose is the correct method for you. Trust in that inner guidance or intuition to lead you in the right direction.

This book will change your life – for the better. If you set your intention and make a choice and commit to taking good care of You, then you will experience life in a brand new way. There are concepts in this book that you've probably heard or read or seen in action before but never actually applied them to yourself or your life. This book is about taking those concepts and beliefs and ways of being and incorporating them into your day to day, moment by moment experience.

You may not feel an affinity for everything I share with you, but, I promise you, you will find something in this book that you can apply today and be the better for it – IF you allow yourself to let this new way of thinking and believing be part of your life.

You're the one who makes that choice, not me. I'm only the emissary, the path-shower, the light bearer, shining a torch on your already trodden path, illuminating it for you. You then choose the next phase of your journey with a bit more clarity and vision and certainty that you're heading in the right direction (as if there could be any other direction).

Here's the caveat, once again: You will gain something positively transformative from this book if and only if, you set your intention and choose to do so with a conviction born deep down in your heart and soul and follow-through with inspired action in your daily life.

As is the case with just about anything there is to learn in life, the choice is yours. I spent more than 30 years going through these various methods because I was so unhappy and I knew there had to be a way to feel better.

I tried the medication path, too, but they just made me feel horrible, upset my entire digestive tract, took away my sex drive, and gave me constipation (and who wants to hold onto that kind of crap on top of feeling like crap?). I'm not saying they won't work for you but they weren't the answer for me.

You obviously have a desire or you wouldn't have read this far. You'll find it helpful to set aside a document, notebook or journal for this journey. You can also pick up *the Go from Frazzled to Fantastic Workbook* on my website: GiaCilento.com. Download it and fill it out on your computer or print it out.

Here's how to get your copy now:

1. Click this link: GiaCilento.com/workbook. You'll see "Get your free downloadable copy of the *Go from Frazzled to Fantastic* .pdf workbook today" and a form to fill out.

2. Add your email address in the first box and your name in the next one, then click on *Get my workbook* button.

3. Watch your Inbox for the confirmation email "Confirmation email and download link from Gia Cilento". Sometimes it goes to Spam so check there if you don't see it within 5-10 minutes.

4. Open it and click on the confirmation link. It'll take you to a download page where you can get your workbook.

5. Give me a shout out Instagram, FB, or Twitter and let me know how you're doing. I'd love to

hear from you - @GiaCilento. I'd love to hear from you.

6. If you're really feeling it, tell your friends.

So, you ready? Well, let's go then.

☺

Part 1

Starting Point

The future can be reprogrammed in this moment.
— Marianne Williamson

Our society doesn't seem set up to facilitate happiness and joy. In fact, having such a strong focus on money and consumption makes it quite difficult.

Is our society set up to make us unhappy? I don't believe it is, but we certainly have a lot of focus on what doesn't work, especially in our media and news channels.

You've probably heard the following phrases: "It's a dog eat dog world." Or, "Every man for himself." (Never mind the women or children). Or, "You can't win for losing." Or, "If life's a bowl of cherries, this must be the pits."

There are dozens or maybe even hundreds of phrases people use to explain away the pervasive feeling of un-joy that they feel. What's your favorite phrase? Shoot me an email and let me know. I'd love to hear it and add it to my collection of *Stuff that just ain't true.*

The question is, in the midst of all this negativity, how do you keep your balance? How do you feel good when there's so much shouting going on about what's bad or what you're missing or what clothes you should wear, what car you should drive, how much money you should make.

It's a wonder we're not at home curled up in bed with the covers pulled over our heads. Though, I admit to having done just that in the past. That's why I had to figure out a way to function, to get to neutral, and then good and then to better. I realized there was more to life and I went after it. Imagine what it would feel like to go through life with the power to hold your own even when the people and environment around you are trying to shake you up?

You don't have to go through life fretting about everything. You don't have to go through life wishing you could just stay home and escape from it all. Joy and happiness are your birthrights – part of your natural state.

So, claim them! Don't let anyone or anything stand in your way. No one has the right to put up roadblocks to your happiness. No one has the right to keep you from creating a world that makes you happy. In reality, no one can actually stop you from being happy unless you allow it.

This book is about claiming your joy and living a fantastic life.

Self-Awareness

Recognizing and Understanding the Current State of Your Inner World

To find that inner state I'm talking about, the state that has you centered and strong, knowing who you are and fully living your fantastic life. To get there, you have to break down the past programming, hurts, wounds, scars, and habitual behaviors that got you to a place where you knew you needed to make a change.

You probably have one or more people in your life who really know how to push your buttons. Sometimes those people are the closest to you, your spouse/significant other (SO), children, closest friend or family; sometimes it's your boss or a co-worker. They know you well and can be your biggest source of irritation at times. They know your buttons and seem to push them whenever possible, purposely or not.

As you go through this course, you'll actually be identifying these buttons and addressing them. Once identified, you can begin the process of dismantling or deactivating them so they're no longer a part of your inner experience.

Talk about freedom! I'm talking about creating the ability to go through life with the power to hold your own even when those around you are trying to shake you up. You can't control them, what they do, what they say, or how they behave, but you can have power over how they impact you.

This process starts with what's going on inside so you can become aware of your current state. Awareness is key in moving your life from where it is to where you want it to be. I guide you to discover what's been in your way and the impact it has on you now and what may lay ahead.

Next, I introduce you to the attributes, ways of being, and some other tools that you'll need to move into a state of inner joy. Then, we look at the practices and habits that help you instill those new states into your life.

Finally, I move you through creating a new set of rituals that propel you forward. Some of the methods may seem a bit out there, woo-woo, or spiritual at first glance. I ask that you be okay with that for a bit. I'm not trying to push any kind of thought form or spiritual belief on you.

These are practices that I've tried and want to pass on to you. Read through their purpose and process and see if there's a way you can fit them into your beliefs. If not, then pass on by and choose another method. Take on the practices that appeal to you and forget about the rest.

Frazzled

You probably picked up this book (or someone gave it to you) because you're in some state of Frazzled – overwhelmed, frustrated, worried, anxious, stressed, pissed off, caught up in negative emotions – and you want to get to some state known as Fantastic. Am I right? I'll take that as a yes.

You might be knee deep in the middle of a career (whether you like it or not) and you know there's either something missing or you're frustrated because you know what's missing from your life, especially from your inner life, and you haven't figured out yet how to get it.

I'm not going to spend a lot of time looking at the present because I'm pretty sure you're aware of how much it sucks, how much you want to change it, or you wouldn't be reading this. However, there are some habitual forms of thought and behavior or ways of being that aren't always known or readily self-identified and they bear some investigation, definition, and awareness.

Self-awareness helps create a foundation for moving your life to a different state, in transforming it into something joyful and fulfilling. To that end, the following section presents some of the most common things people habitually do or think that causes them to feel bad, hate their life, hate people, or make themselves and others miserable.

Let's look at habits of thought, emotions, behaviors, and beliefs that can keep you in a negative state. Take your time considering each item. Make notes on each one you recognize. Consider how you use this in your life to keep yourself spiraling in negativity.

As I said in the introduction, set aside a document, notebook or journal for this journey. Take note if you feel an aversion, nonchalance, or aggravation towards any particular item. That may be something important to investigate even if your initial impulse is to skip it. It may indicate something that lurks in the background of your consciousness, unknown to you.

Make as many notes as possible, especially of any "aha" moments. I've noticed that these discoveries have a way of going into hiding again if they're not documented and available for a second (or third, or fourth) look. This is especially true for those that run in the background or that we turn to when on autopilot.

Stress

You've probably heard that stress is a natural part of life. When occurring in the right dosage and handled with the right mindset, stress is beneficial, helps spur growth and learning and leads to gains in just about all areas of life.

However, when the dosage is too high or the mindset isn't optimal, then stress can trigger a cascade of negative events in life that can impact your health, relationships, body, emotions, career and other areas.

Even situations that most of us would see as "good" cause stress (such as a promotion, getting married, buying a new home, having a baby, etc.) so learning to manage it is an extremely important aspect of life. For many of us, we learn stress-management mechanisms by default as we grow up.

School, in general, teaches us to deal with large numbers of people, being tested, moving from grade to grade, and dealing with obligations, responsibilities, and expectations. These are all stepping stones that teach us stress management skills.

We enter these situations with or without the support of parents, guidance counselors or teachers. There isn't a curriculum set up to teach children how to deal with the stress these different situations and expectation create. We learn to cope on our own and we carry these coping mechanisms with us into adulthood.

What we don't learn, however, is how to deal with life when we're hit with several major stressors at the same time. School is a regimented system. Life is not.

Self-Assessment:

- What's going on in your life right now that you would consider a source of stress?
  - Career?
  - Relationship with Significant Other?
  - Health?
  - Finances?
  - Moving/transferring?
  - Over-commitment?
  - Children issues / parental issues?
- How are you dealing with your stressors?
- What methods do you employ to help manage the stress, deal with it, and use it to help you grow and move forward?

Anxiety/Worry

For our purposes, both of these occur in response to an assumed or imagined negative outcome that is yet to happen though is not guaranteed to happen. Worry is a short-term concentration on the imagined negative future and anxiety is a chronic state of worry.

While it may seem that habitual worry and anxiety are to blame for your unabated levels of stress, these are still symptoms of a collection of habits you've been cycling through. These habits have been around for a long time.

You may have created them out of necessity, to deal with a situation when you were a child, so, they've probably been in use most of your life.

Self-Assessment:

- What aspect of your life has you feeling worried or anxious most often?
- Do you have any control over that area? It's okay if you have more than one area, just write it down.
- When is your anxiety/worry at its highest? Any particular time of day?
- How do you deal with it?
- What physical symptoms do you have when you're most anxious/worried/
- How do you relieve your physical symptoms? Hint: eating, drinking, sexting, shopping?

Complaining

Complaining can take many forms both external or verbal and internal, directed at self or at others. It not only stops the flow of goodness and abundance into your life, its impact expands throughout your life negatively affecting every aspect from love and relationships to career and health.

A complaint and especially habitual complaining put you squarely at odds with having what you want in your life. If you're focused on what you think isn't right or isn't working then you're not really able to see what is working or what is going well. If you're focused on the problem, you're unable to see the solution.

When your mind is filled with complaining thoughts, you usually have a corresponding frown or grouchy face. Your muscles are tense, your circulation is impeded, and you may even trigger your flight or fight mechanism causing your adrenals to ignite. You're not smiling. You're not enjoying yourself. Basically, you're not happy. Your inner world is in a turmoil.

Along with any health implications, you're also ruining your chances at truly enjoying your life, at living a fantastic life. The question to ask yourself: Is it worth it? Take a look at your thoughts and your conversations. How many of them are complaints? When you look at your complaints, are they about a subject you can impact directly or are they about something over which you have no control such as taxes, your neighbor or the weather?

You may have heard of the Serenity Prayer used by Alcoholics Anonymous programs around the world. It puts this aspect into perspective:

Serenity Prayer

God, grant me the serenity to accept the things I cannot change the courage to change the things I can and the wisdom to know the difference

It's time to get real about how much you complain on a daily basis. Your results might surprise you.

Let's take on an experiment and find out:

- How much you complain verbally and internally
- What are your biggest areas of complaint
- If you complain about things you can or cannot control
- What it feels like to be free of complaints

The 10 Day Complaint Free Challenge

For the next 10 days, consider your mind and your mouth to be a Complaint Free Zone. If you find yourself voicing or thinking a complaint, stop and shake your head. Complaining has no place in your joyful world.

- Each morning, set the intention of steering clear of complaints and record in your journal anything that may have occurred to you about making this intention
- Each time you notice you've complained, either in your thoughts or out loud, pause for a second,
- Realize that the complaint had you just put a stop to the flow of happiness within you
- Notice if your pulse or breathing has changed or if there are any other physiological changes
- Take a moment to become fully present to what you just said or thought, then shake it off and replace it with a thought that finds something positive
- Each evening, take note of your experience during the day
  - How often did you find yourself complaining?
  - Did you complain more today than yesterday? Less? Didn't notice?

- o What did it feel like when you realized that you'd stopped your flow of happiness?
- o How was your overall experience throughout the day?
- At the end of the 10-days, examine what changes you've had or made in your day-to-day experience. Do you feel more uplifted? Have you made adjustments in the way you view things? Did you enjoy creating this level of self-awareness?

Let me know how you did with this experiment. Write me @giacilento on Instagram, Twitter or Facebook and let me know what you discover.

Holding Onto Grievances and Events of the Past

When you hold onto the negative aspects of things that happened in the past you keep those things active in your present.

Self-Assessment:

Take some time now to consider what grievances or events from the past you're holding onto. Fill in the blanks here or use your document/notebook/journal.

- I still resent (fill in a person's name) for (fill in the grievance you're holding onto about them).
- I still blame for (fill in a person's name) for (fill in the grievance you're holding onto about them).
- I'm still angry at (fill in a person's name) for (fill in the grievance you're holding onto about them).
- I'm still upset with (fill in a person's name) for (fill in the grievance you're holding onto about them).
- I'm still hurt about (fill in a person's name or the situation).
- I hate (fill in a person's name) for (fill in the grievance you're holding onto about them).

Continue on with these statements until you've filled at least two pages, even if you're repeating yourself or searching for things to say. Take as many pages as you need. If you get tired, take a break and come back to it. Sometimes the deepest issues don't come out until you've exhausted all the overlying ones. You can come back to this exercise time and again until you feel that you've completely let go of everything that had a charge to it.

Blame

Finger pointing, someone else is responsible for how you feel about whatever's going on. There's a need to find a culprit for your feelings, to disown them, not stand in a place of responsibility about your current state.

Self-Assessment:

- I blame (fill in a person's name) for (describe the feeling or situation you're in).
- I blame (fill in a person's name) for (describe the feeling or situation you're in).
- I blame (fill in a person's name) for (describe the feeling or situation you're in).
- I blame (fill in a person's name) for (describe the feeling or situation you're in).
- I (describe the feeling or situation you're in) and it's all your fault!
- I (describe the feeling or situation you're in) and it's all your fault!
- I (describe the feeling or situation you're in) and it's all your fault!

Continue on with these statements until you've filled at least two pages, even if you're repeating yourself or searching for things to say. Take as many pages as you need. If you get tired, take a break and come back to it. Sometimes the deepest issues don't come out until you've exhausted all the overlying ones. You can come back to this exercise time and again until you feel that you've completely let go of everything that had a charge to it.

Anger/Rage

Anger is a natural human response to some situations. There's nothing wrong with feeling anger as long as it's expressed in a way that doesn't bring any harm to oneself or anyone else.

There can be a problem when anger is used to cover up other feelings and not deal with them, such as shame, fear or depression. Or, when anger is unleashed on someone else because you don't know how to handle it properly.

Anger is a feeling you are having, even if someone triggered it within you, it's still your emotion and it's up to you to manage it appropriately and safely.

Rage, on the other hand, is anger on steroids and out of control. Rage is usually directed at someone else and can cause a lot of harm. I consider rage to be a bit beyond the scope of this book though, if you rage, you may find that some of the exercises, particularly meditation, helpful to you.

If you're one whose anger is quick to ignite, you and those around you probably already know it. If you're one to rage, you probably already know this, too. It is possible to handle yourself differently, to release your anger in a way that doesn't hurt anyone else.

Self-Assessment:
Take a good look at what you experience when you're angry.

- What is it that set you off?

- Is anger the usual or common response to this type of event?
- Are you in control of yourself when you feel angry?
- Do you point your anger at someone else to dispel it? Raising your voice? Saying things you'd never say if you weren't angry?
- Do you use your anger as a shield to keep people away from your tender emotions?
- How do you feel after you've had an angry outburst? Relief? Despair? Guilt? Blame? Martyrdom?

Guilt

The other side of the blame game, feeling responsible for someone else's lot in life or emotional state. This isn't about being responsible because the guilt is a mechanism used to keep you in your negative state, keep you embroiled in the drama of whatever situation is at hand and keep you living in the past, upset with yourself.

Self-Assessment:

- I'm so upset with myself because (fill in the blank here) and it's all my fault.
- I'm so upset with myself because (fill in the blank here) and it's all my fault.
- I'm so upset with myself because (fill in the blank here) and it's all my fault.
- I'm so upset with myself because (fill in the blank here) and it's all my fault.

Continue on with these statements until you've filled at least two pages, even if you're repeating yourself or searching for things to say. Take as many pages as you need. If you get tired, take a break and come back to it. Sometimes the deepest issues don't come out until you've exhausted all the overlying ones. You can come back to this exercise time and again until you feel that you've completely let go of everything that had a charge to it.

Martyrdom

A "woe is me, look at how bad my life is, look at how much I have to put up with from (fill in your favorite persecutor)" state. There's a pervasive sense of blame directed at someone who is perceived as persecuting the martyr. They have so much to put up with in life, are so downtrodden and don't mind telling anyone and everyone who will listen. The aim here is to have people see you as someone who has so much to put up with in their lives so you receive sympathy and attention.

Self-Assessment:

Pay close attention when you talk about how bad something is. What words do you use? How often do you talk about it? Do you only talk about it with certain people or when you're feeling a certain way? Try to determine any patterns that you might have around this one.

- Write down what you say or think when you refer to how bad your life is.
- Write down what you say or think when you refer to how bad your job is.
- Write down what you say or think when you refer to how bad your spouse is.
- Write down what you say or think when you refer to how bad your boss is.
- Write down what you say or think when you refer to how bad your parent/sibling/relative is.

Continue on with these statements until you've filled at least two pages, even if you're repeating yourself or searching for things to say. Take as many pages as you need. If you get tired, take a break and come back to it. Sometimes the deepest issues don't come out until you've exhausted all the overlying ones. You can come back to this exercise time and again until you feel that you've completely let go of everything that had a charge to it.

Victim

Similar to the martyr though in a more helpless sense. The victim acts as though things/events just happen to them and they have no say in the matter. As if they're a piece of flotsam bobbing along in the ocean, being bounced about by the waves. There is no sense of responsibility.

It can include behaviors like blame and martyring, hatred and anger. Usually, the person who is seen as the perpetrator isn't there to defend themselves and is painted as wholly bad or evil – no redemptive qualities. It's an all-or-nothing kind of emotion and there isn't usually room for compassion or understanding.

Self-Assessment:
- Pay close attention when you talk about how upset or angry you are with someone or about something.
- What words do you use and with whom?
- Do you complain about how unfair life or a particular situation is?
- Are there certain situations that make you particularly upset or angry?
- Do you only talk about it with certain people or when you're feeling a certain way?
- Try to determine any patterns that you might have around this one.

Continue on with these statements until you've filled at least two pages, even if you're repeating yourself or searching for things to say. Take as many pages as you need. If you get tired, take a break and come back to it. Sometimes the deepest issues don't come out until you've exhausted all the overlying ones. You can come back to this exercise time and again until you feel that you've completely let go of everything that had a charge to it.

Shame

This one is insidious because it's often masked by other feelings of worthlessness, guilt, sorrow or even anger. It's the feeling that you are innately bad and there's no making up for it. There's a sense that you have something to hide and if others found out, they'd revile you and hate you and drive you out of town or try to kill you.

This is a powerful one to uncover. In my experience, it was very difficult to see this aspect. Once I did, however, I realized what a powerful hold it had on me and how much it ran the decisions I made.

Take some time to go through this assessment. You may even need to ask some friends for help. Make sure they're friends who you feel are safe and supportive, not someone who doesn't respect you or your boundaries.

There can be many layers to shame, as there are for most of these programs. If you feel that your sense of shame is deep and you might need more work than is offered here, seek out a coach, spiritual advisor, psychologist or other professional to help you through.

Self-Assessment:

There are physical expressions and interpersonal behaviors that can be an indicator you're harboring internal feelings of shame.

- Hunched shoulders
- Stooping

- Wringing hands or fidgeting when having a conversation
- Not making eye contact, looking at the ground
- Not speaking up for yourself
- Not being able to say no
- Not having good personal and physical boundaries
- Not choosing lovers/partners who are respectful and treat you well
- Search your life and see if you can identify any other behaviors that may indicate there are some issues in this area

Hatred

Hatred is the thought/emotion of extreme dislike towards another, even to the point of wishing them dead. It's the height of ill feelings toward someone else, or even toward your Self. When you engage in hatred you're creating a lot of negative energy and causing harm to yourself.

I've always felt that hatred is a waste of emotion and that it's more harmful to you than it is to the one you hate. There is no good reason to hate. I'm not saying that you should love someone you disdain but if you can refrain from focusing on this extreme, you'll save your energy for your own positive purposes.

You'll release yourself from a negative emotion that could seriously hamper your ability to allow joy into your life. Sustained hatred can also "eat away at you" causing a myriad of physical symptoms.

Self-Assessment:

Look for subjects or people where your feelings of dislike are so intense that you'd call them hate.

- What do these subjects/people represent to you?
- When you think about them, do you have a physical reaction? If so, try to determine what kind of physical reaction you're having. Is it fear? Disgust? Jealousy?
- Be aware of how many times you use the word "hate" during the day. If you notice yourself using it, start to keep track and see how many times. Notice the circumstances where you use

the term. You may start to notice a pattern. Take notes and write about it in your journal.

- Take a fresh look at the areas and people you may currently hate. Is there a possibility of taking your feelings about them to a less severe place? Can you see how your feelings actually impact you physically? Emotionally? Are you willing to at least consider that you're only really hurting yourself by holding onto such strong negative emotions about someone else?

Jealousy

Feeling that someone over there has what you want and deserve. That they have it unfairly and it should be yours. Because they have it and you don't, you resent them and can even hate them.

Self-Assessment:

Look for people you may be jealous of or situations that may ignite your feelings of jealousy.

For example:

- Someone who you think is better looking than you are.
- Someone who appears to have more money than you do.
- A house that is bigger, newer, and grander than yours.
- A person working in the job you think you should have.
- A profession that makes a lot more money than yours and doesn't deserve it.

Think of some examples from your life where jealousy may be lurking, especially look for areas and circumstances where it may be chronic. Then, look to see if that area is going well for you, look to see if your feelings of jealousy are a contributing factor in keeping you from having what you want in that area.

Do you:

- Inflate what you do for a living when you're talking to certain people?

- Feel inadequate physically around certain people?
- Compare yourself unfavorably to some people and more favorably to others?
- Compare yourself and feel superior to some but inferior to others?
- Buy possessions because someone you know has just bought the same thing?
- Flirt with or shun a friend's significant other?

What other behaviors can you pinpoint and identify as coming from a place of jealousy?

Greed

An insatiable desire to have something (money, fame, lovers, food, or any number of things). You want more and are willing to do whatever you have to do to get what you want, lie, cheat, steal, swindle, sometimes even murder.

Self-Assessment:

Look for:

- Areas where you'll stretch or break the boundaries of your honesty and integrity to get what you want
- Situations where you take something or feel tempted to take something that isn't yours
- Situations where you indulge in a sexual relationship with someone – even though you're in a committed relationship.
- Eating or drinking more than you want or need because there's an ample free supply, such as a banquet, smorgasbord, or open bar

The Impact

If you're caught up in any of the above cycles of thought (leading to behavior), you're probably pretty damn-well aware of the impact on your life. You've probably had your share of arguments, failed or damaged relationships, and loss of friends, jobs, fitful nights, and upsetting/anxious mornings.

As you studied these aspects of the human condition, you may have identified pieces of yourself that you were unaware of, ignored, tried to pretend weren't there, were ashamed of or that you felt were warranted. Whatever you took away from this, know that these behaviors exist, in one form/degree or another, in almost everyone.

These emotions and behaviors are part of being human and will probably continue on with us out into the unending future. The question to ask yourself is, "How much will I allow myself to be entrapped by the misery of settling in these emotions."

Let's take anger, for instance. There's nothing wrong with feeling angry. There are times when it's appropriate or unavoidable, say when a hammer falls on your big toe, there's a flash of anger.

What's important, is how you deal with that anger in the moment. Do you lash out at the first unsuspecting passerby, do you hold onto it, allowing it to build into a furnace of rage and then vomit it all over your spouse, or children?

There are other options. What if you tried just acknowledging what you felt, first, taking no action at all? In the case of the hammer on the toe, you might let out a yelp of pain (maybe even with a few curse words thrown in) and hobbled around a while breathing hard and keep it at that. You've safely expressed your anger without pointing it at anyone.

Allowing yourself to sit in any negative state of being on a consistent basis or getting rid of it by dumping it on someone else can have disastrous effects on your ability to cope with life, to have a conversation about something important, to be fit and healthy, to know what you want out of life and to go after it, and to have a loving, nurturing relationship.

Health and Fitness

What is your current state?
What do you want to create in this area?
Go through each item and rate yourself on a scale of 1-10, 10 being the highest. Then take some time to write about which areas might be most impacted by one of the Frazzled behaviors you went through earlier.

Self-Assessment:
- Fatigue
- Stress-related illnesses – high blood pressure
- Chronic depression
- Dis-ease
- Loss of stamina
- Loss of endurance
- Loss of strength
- Decrease in overall ability
- Lack of adaptability
- Loss of sexual desire and diminished performance

Relationships

With spouse/significant other, children, parents, siblings, friends, relatives, co-workers, clients/associates, strangers, humanity in general.

What is your current state?

What do you want to create in this area?

Go through each item and rate yourself on a scale of 1-10, 10 being the highest. Then take some time to write about which areas might be most impacted by one of the Frazzled behaviors you went through earlier.

Self-Assessment:
- Fighting/arguing
- Resentment
- Jealousy
- Rage
- Estrangement

Inner Landscape

What is your current state?

What do you want to create in this area?

Go through each item and rate yourself on a scale of 1-10, 10 being the highest. Then take some time to write about which areas might be most impacted by one of the Frazzled behaviors you went through earlier.

Self-Assessment

- Loneliness
- Worsening state of sadness or depression – downward spiral
- Recreating the same type of event/turmoil over and over
- Certain emotions getting out of control
- Abuse
- Addiction
- Lack of enjoyment of events
- Lack of happiness
- Little or no feeling of fulfillment
- Inner numbness
- Lack of feeling of love and joy

Job/Career

What is your current state?

What do you want to create in this area?

Go through each item and rate yourself on a scale of 1-10, 10 being the highest. Then take some time to write about which areas might be most impacted by one of the Frazzled behaviors you went through earlier.

Self-Assessment:
- Loss of focus.
- Loss of concentration.
- Poor timing.
- No or poor Project Management skills
- Missed promotions
- Missed deadlines
- Poor performance ratings
- Missed raises
- Poor relationships with boss and co-workers
- Arguments or conflicts

Finances

What is your current state?

What do you want to create in this area?

Go through each item and rate yourself on a scale of 1-10, 10 being the highest. Then take some time to write about which areas might be most impacted by one of the Frazzled behaviors you went through earlier.

Self-Assessment:
- Slow bill paying
- Impulsivity
- Spending to feel good
- Gambling (to feel good)
- Inability to save
- Poor credit rating
- Poor investment choices
- Arguments with spouse/SO
- Borrowing money
- Using credit cards to pay regular bills

Choice Point

If you've done the work, you now have a better idea about the impact and the result of allowing this way of being and believing to continue. Now, you get to choose and create a new, self-supportive way to thrive.

There are thousands of different methods out there that you can help you get there. If you were led here it's because this is where you need to be.

Now, it's time to put the blame away, let go of the guilt, stop pointing the finger at other people, or at your boss or at your job or your car or your lawn or your house or your kids or your spouse or the weather.

Just stop!

There's no one else in control of your life but you and when you let go of making your life and your happiness be about how your outside conditions, you will take back control and realize your own power – your power to create the life that you want, to develop yourself into the person you really see yourself being, the person you really are.

Above all, you'll have the power to be there for the people you love as the person you really want to be, the way you know you really want to be there.

☺

Part 2

Creating a Fantastic Life

We are the creative force of our life, and through our own decisions rather than our conditions, if we carefully learn to do certain things, we can accomplish those goals.
— Stephen Covey

Cleaning up your habitual thoughts and subsequent behaviors or your "way of being" is imperative and foundational to purposely create the kind of life you really want. A life you may not have known was available to you. The kind of life you may have thought was a fairy tale where your relationships go well, even through tough times and disagreements. Where you have a supportive circle of friends and family.

Your career is satisfying, fulfilling and moves along at a desirable pace. Your body looks and feels the way you know it should, vibrant, energetic, bouncy, frisky, sexually satisfying and able to handle what comes up in life. And, you wake up in the morning feeling refreshed, happy and excited about what lies ahead.

This type of life takes something unconditional, a way of looking at life and living in this world that doesn't depend on or change based on conditions outside of us. It depends on you making a daily choice to live joyfully and unconditionally. It takes Unconditional Joy.

This life is not a fairy tale. It's yours for the choosing. It's yours to create purposefully. In Part 2 we delve into the underpinnings of a Fantastic Life. We'll explore the "ways of being" that you must embody and cultivate to build your foundation so you can choose unconditional joy every day.

For our purposes, unconditional joy is the inner state of being happy, appreciative, content, and grateful no matter what is going on around us.

Strength and conviction and commitment play a role but what really matters is that you continue to choose your preferred way of being over the habitual way of being you were unknowingly stuck in previously.

Now, let's set up a few parameters so we're on the same page about what joy is all about and, specifically, what unconditional joy is. For our purposes, unconditional joy is the inner state of being purposefully happy, appreciative, content, and grateful no matter what is going on around us.

It's the perception, understanding, acceptance, allowance, and living of the phrase, "It's all good." Literally. It's standing in a place where you're so solidly centered inside that nothing can shake you. The whole world economy could be collapsing around you and you'd still have yourself grounded in that unshakable center.

I don't mean you'd be laughing and wanting to throw a party, I mean you wouldn't succumb to any of the negativity or victim behaviors you may once have. There'd be no blaming, no begging the gods for mercy and wondering why this is happening to you ... again! That's the kind of thinking that leaves you feeling miserable. That's the kind of thinking that keeps you up at night with worry and has you wake up with a belly full of anxiety each morning. It's the kind of thinking that keeps you from getting at a solution and the kind of thinking that keeps you stuck.

Insist on unconditional joy. Make it your way of life for this is a life-changing way of thinking that helps you get through all kinds of times, good and bad, prosperous and lacking, gleeful and sorrowful.

A New Inner You

Gratitude, Love, and Appreciation

Creating a new inner landscape, setting yourself up so you're a responsive, powerful, fulfilled and joyful human being isn't a linear process. I've put together a set of practices, attributes, and behaviors that have helped me Go from Frazzled to Fantastic. I may still have moments where I step back into an old habit of behavior or thought but I don't stay there. Once I recognize it, I pull myself out and realign myself.

As you look through the methods I've laid out, choose what feels right to you in your life, in your mind and heart. Today, that may be a list of two or three and tomorrow or next week, you may add in some and subtract others. There's no right answer on how you get there, as long as you make the commitment to keep reaching for it.

If you can commit to spending time with your Self on a regular basis, whether it's through meditation or journaling or just some alone time taking a bath, you'll send a message to yourself and your family that this is a sacred time. This time you spend focused on your own well-being is incredibly important.

At the foundation of unconditional joy and your peaceful, joyful, happy and fulfilling inner world lies the trifecta of gratitude, love, and appreciation. These three inner states, when chosen and practiced and instilled within you, create your ability to maintain your desired state. You can't complain while you're focused on finding the things you appreciate about something or someone and what you love and are grateful for regarding them. The two things just don't occur together.

Gratitude

Gratitude isn't just something you do, it's something you imbue into your *being-ness*. It's a place to stand in an ever-changing landscape we call life. It's a belief that all is well, life is good, and you are grateful to be breathing this day. When you start from there, you're already in a positive flow. You stand in the center of gratitude and view all the circumstances of living your life from there, from a place of *being in complete gratitude*.

Love

You may have heard that there are a number of ways to say "love" in Latin and other languages. English, however, has only one. One word to describe both the love a couple has, the love for your child, love of a sibling or parent, love for a friend, love for a movie or love for a material object. So many ways love can be expressed and yet we have only the one word to describe them all.

For our purposes, that's okay, because what I'm talking about here is opening and extending your heart, and the feeling you hold in it, out into the world for everyone. This means, sending love to every single human being with no holding back because of their behavior or actions. In fact, those who behave in ways that might upset or take actions that our society might consider "bad" are probably the ones who need our love even more. There has to be a reason, after all, for them to act the way they do.

Appreciation

Appreciation for everything that comes into your life, every circumstance, person, and event. It's there for a reason. It's up to you to determine what that reason may be or to just know and accept it. But holding an appreciation for everything, no matter what, gives you a very powerful place to stand in the world. It gives you your power back. It's you, taking your power back from every little thing that you allowed to bother you in the past.

Think about it. When you combine gratitude, love, and appreciation and you don't discriminate about it, you've just told the entire world that you are in control of your life. You've said that you are the one in charge of how you feel at any given moment; that you determine how you see the world, how you face the world and how you live in the world. You're not at the whim and mercy of every news story or every misdeed, mishap or mistake.

All is well

When you practice gratitude, love, and appreciation and hold it as your foundation, you've formed an unshakable bedrock where unconditional joy can readily flow in, stake a claim and set up residence. When you're living from a place of unconditional joy, no outer condition can rattle you and, if something does upset you, you know you can come right back to center. You bend and sway but you maintain your integrity in the face of whatever comes your way. This may not be a place you arrive right away.

This is a process and you'll see yourself grow and change over time. There will be times you're tested and each one of those times will help you more firmly establish your foundation once you've committed to it.

That's the beauty of creating a solid platform on which to stand and then forming roots on the platform. From here, you develop a deep, inner knowing that all is well, that you can handle life as it comes at you. You develop a deeper sense of confidence and trust. Your sense of self-esteem increases and your ability to take on greater and greater tasks and responsibilities in life expands.

This new way of thinking and new set of beliefs slowly begins to take over your old mindset and replace the old negative self-talk with positive, self-supporting, self-generating thoughts and beliefs.

What It Takes to Create A New Way of Life

You're going to need a toolkit full of new attributes to go along with the new foundation you're creating and the new methods you'll be learning in a little while. Let's take a look at what you'll need within you to take on your new way of life and make it stick. After all, you don't want this to be some random failed experiment.

You want that new way of life. You know you want to wake up in the morning feeling good about who you are. You also know that you'll have to give up playing the victim, placing blame, getting angry at life or your spouse or your boss, or whatever crutch you use to keep yourself in a crappy place. For some people, like me, this might be easier said than done.

Let's face it, you wouldn't be acting that way if you didn't get something out of it. Breaking that habit takes self-awareness and a commitment to getting where you want to go. This is where you may have to resort to some good old-fashioned a-- kicking to keep yourself on track.

How to Kick Your Own A — and Still Have Fun

There will be times when you're tempted to resort to your old habits. When this happens, you have to stop yourself, remember who you are and where you're going and move forward.

When you find yourself falling into some old habits and/or old behaviors, you're going to have to brush off some attributes that might be a bit dusty, like your courage, integrity, honesty, trust, honor, commitment and truthfulness.

Most of all, you have to brush off your sense of humor and ability to have fun.

As we move forward and look at these attributes, you may have some "aha" moments or realizations on just how poorly you've been doing at keeping your word and doing what you say you're going to do. You may realize that you've been far too serious and hard on yourself. You've taken pot-shots at your self-esteem and rarely allow yourself to have fun or laugh.

Don't get all upset, though. Take a look around. This is the water we're all swimming in. How often do you hear people talk about honor and integrity anymore? Or courage, honesty, trust, commitment, truthfulness? Who talks about these things in a public forum, or at home, or with friends?

How often does our news talk about how upstanding someone is, especially a public servant, or how loving they are or funny (except professional comedians) and how well they're doing in their lives?

So, if these attributes aren't where they could be in supporting your life, it's not a surprise. The good news is that it's all within your control. Having honor, being honest or trustworthy or courageous, having integrity and sticking to your commitments, laughing and having fun while you go through your day, these are things that are within your reach.

You just have to want them, you have to want to taste the freedom of your new way of life and crave it more than you want the familiarity and sameness of your old way.

So, let's put some definitions and examples around each of these attributes. Then, you'll know when you're on point or off track. Don't make it a point of worry or concern, though. You're going to have times when you're not in alignment. Expect it, acknowledge it, and get right back on that path once you've recognized it.

Also, there may be times when you don't recognize it yourself. Then, something happens that taps you on the shoulder and lets you know you're off your path. If you can hear it at this level, you can step right back where you want to be. At other times, you may not hear the tap on your shoulder and then you end up with a slap across the face. It doesn't feel good but it snaps you out of your old habit, your old autopilot, and wakes you up again. That's okay, too.

If you can look at it, even when it feels uncomfortable, and know that it's part of the process, you'll be that much better equipped and practiced to stick with this new path you've chosen. The more you practice, the better you'll get at recognizing it and the better you'll be at snapping back into alignment with your inner goals.

Of course, just like you, I'm not on point all the time. I do my best but sometimes I just slip into overwhelm – as I did while putting this book together, or anger – as happens at times when I'm driving in traffic and someone cuts me off or nearly takes off my front bumper. If you want to test yourself, go ahead and purposely get on the road during rush hour. Driving is a great way to hone your skills, just try not to flip anyone off while you're out there practicing.

Remember, we're all in this together so the better we get along, the better life will be for everyone. Over time, your propensity to react to the actions of other driver's decreases and your ability to simply enjoy your drive, no matter the traffic or behavior of other drivers, increases greatly.

There are self-assessment questions with each of the attributes. Use your journal to write your answers. Be as honest as you can be with yourself. Come back and re-do this section as you move forward so you can keep track of your progress. You'll notice movement over time and that helps keep you moving forward.

Commitment

When you commit to creating a better life for yourself, you've made a promise. You'll need the self-discipline to stand by your word. Commitment gives you a powerful place to stand with respect to the promise you've made to yourself (and to your loved ones, by default).

Commitment is something that you develop as a skill over time. The more commitments you notice you keep, the more your confidence builds. Take note of all the commitments you already keep such as the chores you do around your house, showering, brushing your teeth, doing laundry, taking out the garbage.

These are all learned activities that you had to make a commitment to do at one time. Look around and give yourself a boost by realizing just how many commitments you already carry out with ease, then take the self-assessment below.

Self-Assessment:
- What is your definition of commitment?
- How do you express your commitment currently?
- Do people in your life, especially your loved ones, believe you when you make a commitment to them?
- Do you break your commitments often?
- Do you keep the commitments you make to yourself?

- What else do you notice about your approach and management of your commitments?

Honesty, Integrity, Truth

These are combined together because they work interchangeably and synchronistically. In our context, they refer to your relationship with your word. Saying what you mean and meaning what you say.

Being consistent in keeping your word to others and in this context, especially to yourself. If you aren't honest with yourself and if your word has no meaning to your subconscious mind, then how can you expect to make any changes in your life and have them stick?

You must be nakedly honest with yourself. From there, you have the ability to be vulnerable and maintain your integrity. You create a real truth about your inner world.

You're aware and alert to what you're feeling so you can direct your emotions in real time, being responsive, not reactive. You have the ability to choose, within moments, how to interpret what's going on and deal with it on your own terms.

When you allow honesty, integrity, and truth into your life, purposefully and powerfully, you create trust.

Self-Assessment:
- On a scale of 1-10, 10 being the highest, what is your level of:
    o Trustworthiness
    o Honesty
    o Integrity
- Do you think others believe you would do the right thing in a vital situation?

- Do you readily trust others?
- Do you trust too quickly and without real awareness, getting yourself into situations that don't serve you well?
- Would you do the right thing even if you knew you could do whatever you wanted and no one would ever find out?
- Do you do the right thing when no one is looking?
- Do you keep your promises to your Self? To others?

Courage

You'll need to shore up your courage if you're going to be nakedly honest with yourself. It can get messy and even painful when you come face to face with your own inner workings, some of which have led to failures in relationship or career or friendship. Some of which have led to behaviors and actions you'd rather forget.

But, that's no reason to hide away. In fact, it's even more reason to push forward. That's where courage comes in. You'll use it to push through any pain or shame or remorse you may feel as you make your way through this course.

It takes courage to stay the course and be true to yourself, to the desires of your heart for a full, vibrant, joyful life. Courage is moving forward in the face of fear and resistance.

You already have courage. That's what had you choose this book. That's what has you keep going every day. It takes courage to keep going in the face of anxiety and worry and the unknown. If you've failed in the past, face it and let it go.

In reality, there's no point to carrying around anything from the past, especially shame, guilt, or remorse. Whatever happened, it happened in the past. Let's have it stay there.

If you feel you're lacking in courage, start building up that muscle by giving yourself one new task each week that stretches you, just a little. If you're afraid to talk to people you don't know yet, practice saying hello to someone passing by. Keep trying until you've accomplished it.

Then, select a new target, to use the same example, your next step would be to say hello to someone who you have to be around for a bit, like the cashier at the grocery store or the person sharing an elevator with you.

Self-assessment:

- On a scale of 1-10, 10 being the highest, what is your level of Courage?
- Think of the last time you did something even though you were afraid to do it.
- How do you react when someone approaches you with something new to do, an activity or a team they want you to join?
- Do your responses help you move forward or keep you standing still?

Discipline

In this case, I'm talking about honoring your commitment to the training and practice necessary to achieve the new way of life you've chosen. You'll have to meet and resist your desire to stay the way you are, to watch TV when it's time to meditate, blame your boss when you don't get the promotion, or to feel guilty when you take time for yourself to practice.

Now, discipline is an ally in your quest for a Fantastic Life. The goal is to instill within yourself a sense of unconditional joy and maintain it no matter what. That's really the main discipline you need to apply.

Remember, you're working to acquire an entirely new set of habits, skills, beliefs so be patient with yourself. Allow yourself enough time and space to go through whatever you have to go through, to tackle whatever comes up and to wrestle with the demons that you might expose.

It takes some time to create a new habit. I've heard time spans from 21 days to 60 or even 90 days. For me, the most critical time is the first 2-3 weeks. That's the time when you're trying to put in the new habits and the old habits are trying to stick around.

This is the time when you'll have to exert the most courage, discipline, commitment, and integrity. If you miss a day, or even two or three, put everything you have into getting back on course and following through. Don't waste time or energy beating yourself up. Put it in the past and start fresh. Just take it one day at a time and one step at a time.

Congratulate yourself each step of the way. Celebrate your victories and reward yourself when you've made it through the first three weeks. Then keep right on going for another three weeks.

Keep going until you've reached the 30-day mark and take another assessment. Then, again on day 60 and day 90. See where your levels are after each time period. From then on, you may want to assess quarterly and move out to every six months and then annually.

Self-assessment:

- On a scale of 1-10, 10 being the highest, what is your level of Discipline?
- Do you have a set ritual that you perform everyday/morning/evening?
- Do you currently have an exercise regimen you perform regularly?
- Do you find it difficult to get up in the morning or to go to bed at a particular time?
- Do you have any preconceived notions about the word "discipline"? Does it bring up any unpleasant memories or situations?
- Does the thought of being disciplined bring you any physical or emotional discomfort?

More Tools for Your Journey

Active Listening

This happens when you allow yourself to be fully present with another such that you're intently focused on what they're saying, what their body language is saying and what their intention is. Your thoughts are still and you're absorbing what they're communicating. Your full attention is upon them.

When you give your full attention to another in this way, you create a bridge between you that allows a fuller experience of relationship. If you've had or currently have a relationship with someone that's important to you, learning, practicing and applying this skill will help you take that relationship to new levels of love, trust, joy, appreciation, and understanding.

Self-Assessment:

- On a scale of 1-10, 10 being the highest, what is your level of listening?
- What kind of a listener are you?
- Do you know what you're going to say before the other person finishes their sentence?
- Do you interrupt people?
- Do you have arguments, disagreements or misunderstandings often?
- Do people come to you for advice?
- Do you pay close attention to what the other person is saying, making eye contact as often as possible?

Release unnecessary expectations of yourself and others

Holding unnecessary, narrow, or unrealistic expectations, whether conscious or subconscious, of yourself or others, can set you up for disappointment, frustration, and conflict. It can also prevent you from recognizing when/if the outcome occurs in a different way.

For example, if you have an expectation that your soul mate will be 6' tall, with black hair and green eyes, you may miss the opportunity of a great love with the one who's 5'10" with brown hair and brown eyes.

Or, you have an expectation that you would look best if you were 100 lbs. lighter but in reality, you would be a stick figure at that weight. If you hold onto this expectation and don't see yourself objectively (or as objectively as possible) you'd miss the admiring looks and glances you receive when you've lost 60 lbs. and reached an ideal weight for your height and build.

Or, you may have a mate who you want to be more responsible about money. You have a specific expectation that this means your mate will begin to shop only on sale days and will use coupons on a regular basis. You may miss the new behavior that has your mate setting a budget and sticking to it, decreasing impulse buys and planning purchases in advance.

If you hold a set expectation, you'll miss the new behavior and your mate will feel unappreciated while you feel disappointed, your stress will continue to build because you think the money problem is still present and you'll continue to worry. Your relationship is strained and more problems arise as conflict mounts Keep your eyes open for the areas where you may have expectations that are fixed, rigid, unrealistic or unnecessary. Use the following questions to help you determine where you're holding expectations that are causing you undue stress and worry.

Self-Assessment:

The following questions will help you see where you're holding expectations of others that are probably going to cause you stress, anxiety, worry or anger/frustration of some sort.

- Do you think other people should behave a certain way? Do you get upset when they don't?
- Do you think your spouse/children/co-workers are pulling their weight? Do you think they should be doing something differently?
- Do you believe there's only one way to do certain things and get upset when others don't do it that way?
- Do you believe that there are a lot of people who just don't have "common sense"?
- Do you decline to participate in new activities because you don't think you'll be good at it? Believing that you *should* know how to do something even though you've never tried it before is an expectation of yourself.

- Do you expect yourself to be perfect? Do you expect perfection from others, especially spouse/children?

Set goals/desires that propel you forward

Having a goal/desire and a purpose in life can be the most fruitful and joyful experience. Knowing the difference between a goal/desire and a fantasy is important. A goal is something you move toward while a fantasy, for our purposes, is something that stays beyond your reach, a pipedream.

There are many methods for goal setting and you may have used some of them through your work or other avenues. The thing to remember is to have goals that make you reach out for them and that the achieving of them is something you can believe in your heart and mind.

For example, if you set a goal to become a pitcher for the NY Yankees yet don't have an inner belief that the goal is achievable by any stretch of the imagination because you're 45 years old, out of shape, and haven't pitched a ball since you were 13, you've set yourself up for failure and the thing you wanted to achieve will remain a fantasy.

Holding and moving toward a goal or purpose that has you jumping out of bed in the morning full of focus and excitement and anticipation is life-giving. Pining after an unachievable, unrealistic and unfulfilled fantasy causes stress, fatigue, and even depression.

Self-Assessment:
- Do you purposefully set goals for yourself?
  - Are your goals well thought out and planned?

- o Do they have a start and end date?
- o Do they cause you to stretch and go beyond what you've achieved in the past?
- o Are they within the realm of possibility to achieve?
- o Does the thought of achieving your goal/desire bring you joy?

- Do you have any active daydreams that occupy your attention?
- Do you have a vision for your life that you're actively moving toward?
- Do you actively seek to identify and address problems in your life by devising a solution and creating a plan to make it happen?
- Look through your life for unmet goals or dreams that you've continued to hold onto even though they are no longer possible to achieve and/or would no longer serve you in the grander scheme of your life.
- Look through your life for unmet goals, desires or dreams that you've put them on the back-burner for one reason or another. Take another look at them and assess the possibility and probability of finding a solution or creating a plan to achieve them now.

Celebrate Your Victories, Milestones, and Accomplishments

Give yourself at least a moment of acknowledgment when you've reached a milestone or reached a goal or overcome something from the past. They're everywhere along your path of life so look for them, especially the small ones as they are the building blocks.

Taking time to acknowledge where you are on your path and appreciate everything that you've accomplished, however small, puts you in the mindset of appreciation on a regular basis. When you have the mindset of appreciation and you pour out gratitude for life, you build the momentum for receiving more and more of the same.

Self-Assessment and practice:

- Look through your life and notice where you've moved past a perceived obstacle, accomplished a goal, achieved some form of success and list them out in your journal.
- Write down 3-5 items from the day that you can celebrate as an accomplishment, a victory over the past, a milestone or some reason for you to feel excited about your achievement
- Repeat this process at the end of every day and include in your journal
- On a regular basis, take time to focus your attention on your achievements, acknowledge them, appreciate what you've gained from them

How to Go From Frazzled to Fantastic

and feel the satisfaction and gratitude of attaining them
- Realize that every day you have several achievements you can claim.

70

Volunteer, Give, Be Generous

Be in service to someone else or a group of someone else's, it doesn't have to be formal. Help the person with a cast on their leg get their groceries, tidy up your neighbor's yard if they aren't able, leave a dollar or a $5 bill at the gas pump next time you're there, think of something you can do to help or share your love and good inner feelings with someone and it will amplify your vibration and your good feeling energy high for days.

Self-Assessment:

- Have you ever volunteered before or do you do so regularly?
- Have you made regular donations to a charity or church?
- If you've never volunteered to help at a local charity, church, hospital, soup kitchen, elderly facility, or something similar, schedule a time to do so. Make note of how you feel before, during and after.
- Pay it forward – do something kind for someone without any expectation of receiving acknowledgment or reciprocation whatsoever. Note how you feel about it, the feeling of giving unconditionally, no strings attached.
- Make giving and helping others a habit in your life.

☺

Part 3

Inner Preparation

To forgive is to set a prisoner free and realize that prisoner was you. – Lewis B. Smedes

Your inner life sets the stage for and creates how you interact with your outer life. For example, let's say you're feeling cranky and you get on the road on your way to work. You'll very likely run into all the a--holes out there.

Along the way, you'll get stuck in traffic, no matter how early or late you leave. Someone or more than one someone is going to cut you off, flip you off or piss you off and you're going to get to work feeling angry, frustrated and drained.

Then, the parking lot will be full and you'll have to park out in BFE. You'll drop your briefcase and all your papers will fall out, into a puddle. Or, you'll break a heel, tear your coat, slam the door on your finger or some other ridiculous nonsense that puts you over the edge. Finally, you get to your desk and you're ready to scream, cry, choke someone, fall apart, or turn around and go home.

If you've ever had to go to work in the morning, (or evening or at midnight) you've probably had one or more days like this. You were probably running a bit late, were a bit distracted, thinking about that thing you still needed to do or that deadline that you're about to miss or the argument you had with your offspring or that date that didn't go nearly as well as you'd have liked.

So, let's rewind a bit and see what happens when you take a bit of time, even a few minutes, to pray or meditate or hum your favorite song in the shower while you're getting ready. You take a moment, smell that pretty bouquet of flowers you remembered to get yourself the night before and you spend 15 seconds smiling at yourself in the mirror, saying "I love you", then sit quietly and meditate for 10-15 minutes before you get dressed.

In other words, you set yourself up for a smooth transition from home to car to work. You were present enough to give yourself the gift of the moment, of creating a clear mind and you paved the way for a smooth travel period. You chose what clothes you'd wear the night before and prepped your breakfast and lunch – for yourself and anyone else who relies on you for their morning and midday meals. When you got on your way, you may have even turned on some tunes – not the news but you had a playlist already put together that, again, set you up for the win.

You gave yourself a gift and transformed yourself from the person you are behind closed doors, in the privacy and sanctity of your own home, to the persona you put on when you're in public and at work. It's a big transition. It takes place while you're hurtling through space in your vehicle, surrounded by about a ton of metal and other material. It happens every day and yet it's overlooked, under-recognized and barely even acknowledged as something meaningful that can and often does impact the rest of your day.

So, when you take the time to focus your attention on your Self for even a few moments each day, with intention and purpose, you pave the way for a smooth run. You create an environment within that is conscious and serene, active and happy. In this state, even if someone did cut you off while you were driving, you wouldn't care, in fact, you may not even notice it because you're sailing along full of happiness. You're not sitting on the bumper of the car in front of you wondering why the hell they're going so slowly.

This section presents a variety of methods, actions, and practices you can use to help you get where you've decided to go.

Let it be Easy

This is something that I've actually used as a mantra in my life. It's made a huge difference to me when I've been faced with something that seemed difficult.

So, use it. Paint it on your wall. Write it on sticky notes and put them everywhere. This is a come from, a mental state or filter you willingly and purposefully put over your eyes that helps everything else flow. Life doesn't have to be hard.

Sure, sh!t happens, but who cares? It's in the past, right? (Thank you, Lion King, for such a wonderful visual of this. If you don't know what I'm talking about, watch the movie.) What's important is what kind of person you are in the face of it all. How do you handle yourself? Do you break down? Throw a tantrum? Yell and scream at people?

Or, do you look at the situation, assess any possible damage, and then switch into solution mode and try to figure out what to do next and where to go from there? I'm not saying you won't shed a tear or be upset or get angry. I'm saying that, in the face of those emotions, you'll acknowledge them, acknowledge the problem and then switch right into solution mode.

You've taken the time to work through the first half of this book. Now it's time to figure out who you want to be from now on.

Are you the person who melts or the person who rebuilds? Are you the person who condemns or the person who creates bridges?

When I was a kid we were on a cross-country trip from Michigan to Florida. There were six of us in the car, five kids, and my Mom. Mom is an amazing lady. Growing up, I admired her for her grace, beauty, and strength. There were times when I was in awe of her and how she managed to deal with my father (a man who had some serious mental health problems) and raise five children in a foreign country. She's from Australia so she did all this with no network of family support or even advice.

So, we were on a trip to Florida, stopped in Tennessee to visit some friends and got lost on the country roads. We stopped somewhere to ask for directions and the man told us, "Well, ya cain't get there frum here." He wasn't very helpful initially but we finally found our way to our destination. Looking back later, that phrase had us all laughing for the delivery and meaning of it and it stuck with me.

To me, it's very apropos of the principle, Let it be Easy. If you're stuck in the emotion and drama/trauma of your problem, you can't see the solution, even if it's staring you in the eye. "Ya just can't get there from here."

The problem creates physical and mental reactions, chemicals are released, certain brain receptors are awakened, and synapses are traveling down paths of alert and alarm. Fight or Flight may be triggered creating a cascade of physical and neurological reactions. All this can happen in a split second.

The solutions, on the other hand, paves the way for jumping from reactive to responsive in a matter of moments. It takes practice, but it's doable. Yes, adrenaline will still be coursing through your body, but you'll be able to harness it and use it to help you think even more clearly and come up with even better solutions.

When you choose to *Let it be Easy*, practice it and allow ease to flow through your life, you create a brand new way of looking at situations.

Energy/Vibration and Resonance

I'm not a physicist but I believe Einstein and others when they say that all matter is energy, that all matter is vibration. Frankly, it's not something that I fully grasp and it's beyond the scope of this book. I'm okay with that, frankly.

I know that there are thousands of functions going on in my car that I can't explain but I still know how to operate it. I also know that it needs proper attention to run smoothly and efficiently, that it needs the proper fuel, oil, transmission and other fluids or it will burn up inside and stop functioning.

So, there are certain things about who we really are deep down and how we really function that makes sense to bring forth. Since all matter is vibration, and we are made up of matter, then it stands to reason that we are vibration or energy. We are energy, as is everything else that exists.

All our senses are actually interpreters of vibration of specific frequencies. Our eyes see a certain spectrum that we translate to red, orange, yellow, green blue, indigo, or violet. You already knew this, didn't you? You just didn't realize that it meant your eyes are interpreters of vibration that has a certain frequency.

And, your ears? Well, they have a certain spectrum of interpretation, too. You see the trend here, yes? Extended to touch, smell and taste, the implications are clear. We are interpreting all the time. And, we are translating those interpretations, filtering them through our belief systems, determining if what we see, hear, smell, touch, taste belongs within our accepted parameters or if it doesn't fit and, therefore, must be discarded or feared.

The translation and filtering process is almost instantaneous and it's the place where there is room for much juicy transformation. This is the place where you may ask what or who is doing all the actual interpreting and filtering. Who decided on those filters? Well, that's the big question, isn't it? Is it merely a bunch of synapses firing in our brain or is there order and sense out of the chaos of happenings that occurs somewhere else. Is there a mind behind the machine?

That's definitely a bit too broad a subject for this book, but the idea that there is a something doing the interpreting gives us the concept that we have a say over the way we choose to interpret those signals once we've received them.

Most of our filters just happened along the way of living our lives as we experienced different events and found ways to deal with them. Some were placed there through training by parents and teachers and society. Others were more conscious choices as we grew older and decided that this worked better than this, that this was good and this other thing was bad.

Regardless of how they got there, there is layer upon layer of filters in place that guides your interpretations and has you seeing things in a certain way. Our goal here is to install some new habits that help you get underneath some of those filters and create a place where you're choosing how you feel inside from moment to moment. These new habits help you interpret what's going on around you from a perspective of mindful purpose with the focus on your own sanctity as a being, the conscious creation of your experience and that what's going on around you is just … something that's going on around you.

You become a bit more detached from the goings on in the world and, therefore, less impacted on a moment by moment, emotional basis. You realize that everyone is going about creating their own reality and that you have the power and the responsibility to intentionally create yours, too.

You come to a place where you see that what's going on around you has to do with that person's filters and interpretations and that other person's filters and interpretations, and so on. Billions of people throughout our planet creating their own reality and filtering their circumstances through their own unique layers.

When you detach yourself from everyone else's creations, you create freedom. You create a clean platform from which you can pick and choose what you want in your life.

Breath = Life

It may sound elementary yet it's fundamental to life as well as relaxation and stress relief. When you're tense and stressed, you take shallow breaths. Your brain, muscles, and cells don't get an adequate supply of oxygen and you stop functioning properly. Your thinking is muddled and your body eventually becomes ill.

Breathing is normally automatic yet you can focus your attention on breathing and train yourself to breathe optimally. Take longer, slower, deeper breaths using your diaphragm, the muscles that run along the bottom of your lungs horizontally across and through your body. You'll know you're doing this when you see your abdomen move in and out instead of your ribs or shoulders.

Breathing properly will enhance every aspect of your day. You'll automatically put your shoulders back more to properly fill your lungs. After you eat, make sure to take some time to relax and breathe so your digestive system has enough oxygen to work properly. When you meditate, breathe in for a count of three and out for a count of five in a relaxed manner.

During your moment-by-moment activities, check in every so often on how you're breathing. You may have to consciously tell yourself to breathe. For a time, I had stickies in various parts of my home and on my computer reminding me to do so. You may find this a helpful practice while you create this new habit of taking longer, deeper breaths.

Choose Your New Practices/Habits

Let's turn our attention, now, to choosing the new habits we want to install in our lives, on purpose. There are probably hundreds of different methods for creating an inner world that you love, based on unconditional joy. When I first started writing this section, I had a huge list of techniques that I've tried over the years.

Once I started adding in the How to descriptions I realized that there were far too many to describe adequately in one book. So, I narrowed it down to what worked best for me and what I believe are the essentials. These are techniques and skills that I've used to help break through some of my unknown filters and ones that I continue to use on a daily basis now.

After more than 30 years of learning and searching for what works and what doesn't, I've found the following to be the most effective methods for reaching a state of inner calm, peace, and quiet. From that place, freedom is within your grasp, the whole world opens up to you in a whole new way.

Meditate

I'm sure I'd heard of meditation long before I was formally introduced, though, at this point, I don't really remember. I can't tell you the year, but it was sometime in the mid-80's. My sister, Abby, took me to a friend's house to meditate.

"You have to come, Gi, it's the most amazing thing. You'll love it," she said.

So, I went. What else can you do? When you sister wants you to go somewhere with her, you go. I didn't know what to expect and I was nervous. At that time, meditation wasn't as well-known as it is now. More to the point, it was a big unknown to me but I was willing to give it a try. In the back of my mind, I remember thinking that I would find out I'm some kind of meditation prodigy. I'd always wanted to be a prodigy of some kind, but meditation wasn't it.

It's not that meditation is hard, it's not. It's that it takes getting used to, at least it did for me. I'd like to say that I created a practice from there that I maintained throughout my life but it wasn't that cut and dry. It was an amazing introduction and I enjoyed myself but I didn't go back right away.

I had other things going on, after all, and was full of excuses. I did meditate again, eventually, after finding out more about it and hearing it from several other sources. I found some tools to help me get past my stubborn resistance, some books I read that explained more about it, and finally, some guided meditations that helped me focus my mind, still my thoughts and a still, calm place within me.

Meditation is the key to cut through the chatter of your brain. There's a seemingly endless loop of bits and pieces of conversation, verses from songs that play over and over, Mom or Dad yelling at you for something you did wrong when you were 5 years old. Take a moment, close your eyes, and see if you can hear it running in your head right now.

Meditation helps you set aside all those thoughts and get to the quiet places that are hiding just beyond. This is your access to that still, small voice, the voice or sense or knowing place that's the door to that greater part of all of us, to God. Through meditation, you realize you're an integral part of this greatness, loved beyond all knowing, supported and cared for and tended to, whether or not you can see it and feel it and hear it and touch it and taste it.

In fact, you find that your senses sometimes get in the way of actually aligning with this greater part. Meditation helps you go beyond your five senses. You slow your mind and access the part of you that is the thinker of your thoughts and dreamer of your dreams. It is your access to the unconditional outlook you need for unconditional joy.

There are meditation workshops, Meetups, classes and gatherings popping up all across the country. If this is something you're interested in, take a moment and Google groups in your area or on Meetup and join them.

I created a guided meditation that you can download from my website at GiaCilento.com/meditation.

In your journal ask yourself:

- When you think of this method, do you have any physical reaction, pleasant or unpleasant?
- Do you have any prior experience with this method? If so, can you set aside that past experience and have a fresh look at it?
- Take a few moments to contemplate this method and consider if you'd like to try it now or set it aside for now and come back to it later?

Pray

Prayer is your time to send up to God or whatever higher power you believe in (even if it's You) the things you want to create or change in your life. Prayer is a powerful ally in your journey unconditional joy and creating the inner world that you desire.

To me, prayer is not about begging or demanding or asking to win the lottery. Those are the types of prayers that come from a victim mentality, a belief in scarcity and a belief that what happens in your life comes from outside you, that you have no say in the matter.

When you stand in a place of power and strength and knowing inside, you understand that you create what comes to you. From this viewpoint, prayer is about receiving clarity, understanding what you've already created, and creating a vision for the next part of your journey.

In your journal ask yourself:

- When you think of this method, do you have any physical reaction, pleasant or unpleasant?
- Do you have any prior experience with this method? If so, can you set aside that past experience and have a fresh look at it?
- Take a few moments to contemplate this method and consider if you'd like to try it now or set it aside for now and come back to it later?

Smile

This may seem too simple, but this is a powerful partner in creating the inner world of joy and happiness that you seek. Try it. Just put a smile on your face whenever you think of it for the next 24 hours and see what a difference it makes. Notice how people treat you differently when you approach them with a smile.

It even makes a difference over the phone, when you're texting or writing an email. When you smile as you perform these tasks, your voice sounds different, your tone is different and it comes across on the other end. Plus, it's contagious, just like yawning and laughing.

In your journal ask yourself:

- When you think of this method, do you have any physical reaction, pleasant or unpleasant?
- Do you have any prior experience with this method? If so, can you set aside that past experience and have a fresh look at it?
- Take a few moments to contemplate this method and consider if you'd like to try it now or set it aside for now and come back to it later?

Laugh

This one goes right along with smiling. Laughing makes you feel better. It's contagious. Try listening to a group of people, better yet a baby, laughing and you'll find yourself laughing right along with them.

I was part of a team of people who were putting on a training course many years ago. At our first meeting, our team captain told us we were going to do a group meditation. He had us all lie down on the floor in a circle with our heads facing the center of the circle. Once we were in position, he told us that the entire meditation was going to be laughing. There were some nervous chuckles and some disbelieving murmurs at first because it sounded a little ludicrous, even to those of us who already meditated. It didn't seem serious enough.

He started the laughter and I joined in because I'd been told to do so. Within a minute, I felt myself relaxing and really laughing. There was no comic around, no one telling funny stories, just the laughter of others around me and my own laughter. Pretty soon, everyone was rolling on the floor literally belly-laughing. It was one of the most exhilarating experiences I've ever had which is why the story made it to this book. Our team was successful, too, cohesive, in-sync, and responsive.

Try it at home by yourself or with a partner and test it out for yourself. Set a time limit, say 5 minutes then write down your thoughts and reaction.

In your journal ask yourself:

- When you think of this method, do you have any physical reaction, pleasant or unpleasant?
- Do you have any prior experience with this method? If so, can you set aside that past experience and have a fresh look at it?
- Take a few moments to contemplate this method and consider if you'd like to try it now or set it aside for now and come back to it later?

Reiki

When I was a teenager, I actually healed myself of some scratches my little sister left on my hand with nothing but my thoughts. I was young enough to try it but old enough to be a bit jaded and think it was a fluke.

Fast forward a few years (okay, a lot of years) to the time I first learned Reiki. I think it was early 1998. I ended up taking a Reiki Level I course in May and a week or two later I was involved in a bad car crash that left me virtually flat on my back for months. I was in different types of therapy for a couple of years and on a reduced schedule at work, too.

I'd always known, deep down, that I had an ability to heal myself. I just wasn't sure how to tap into it. Now I found myself in a situation where I really needed to find a way to heal. I had to get back on my feet, literally, and live my life again.

So, I tried it. I used Reiki to help myself heal and it helped - a lot, and I knew that I wanted to continue on with it. I took Reiki Level II and, later, I became a Reiki Master/Teacher. Eventually, between the therapy, my commitment, my daily Reiki, and meditation, I was able to walk again almost as if nothing had happened. I still get aches and pains occasionally and I continue to use Reiki and meditation to help me relieve them.

The word Reiki combines two Japanese words - Rei which means "God's Wisdom or the Higher Power" and Ki which is "life force energy". So Reiki is actually "God or spiritually guided life force energy." I've been a Reiki Master / Teacher for nearly 20 years and I've trained a lot of people in this gentle healing modality including doctors and nurses.

I believe we're all born with the ability to heal ourselves and, after learning about Reiki, I knew that what I'd discovered as a teen was right on point. We can heal our bodies, given the right guidance, focus, and support. Reiki is about re-establishing our innate energy flow/connection and returning our bodies to the natural healing miracles that they were designed to be.

Perfect health is our natural state and Reiki helps facilitate a return to that state. The more you practice Reiki the stronger the energy flow becomes. Reiki helps with all the levels of a human being including body, emotions, mind, and spirit. The effects can range from relaxation to healing, from spiritual connection to freedom from old emotional wounds.

In your journal ask yourself:

- When you think of this method, do you have any physical reaction, pleasant or unpleasant?
- Do you have any prior experience with this method? If so, can you set aside that past experience and have a fresh look at it?
- Take a few moments to contemplate this method and consider if you'd like to try it now or set it aside for now and come back to it later?

Gratitude Journal

This is an exercise in activating and building your gratitude muscle by recognizing and acknowledging all that you have to be grateful for on a daily basis. Set a time period, anywhere from two weeks to 2 months (more if you're so inclined and enjoying yourself), choose a time of day that works best – morning or before bed, and write a daily list of at least 10 things you're grateful for.

There are no limits here. It's not just about the material or your close relationships, but about the everyday occurrences that mostly go unnoticed. It's the breath you just took; the robin you just saw fly across your yard; the leaf that fell so gently to the ground; the sound of the wind in the trees and a thousand other things.

It's also about the things that you might otherwise think of as "bad" like getting stuck in traffic or that relationship that didn't work out, try though you might. Is there possibly a silver lining? A reason underlying the set of circumstances that you just don't have the perspective to see just yet? Maybe getting stuck in that traffic jam caused you to avoid a crash?

Maybe having the door shut on that relationship caused you to look at a pattern you'd unknowingly created in your behavior, something that you could now address and make yourself ready for an even better relationship. These are also things you can put down in the gratitude column.

Questions to ask yourself:

- When you think of this method, do you have any physical reaction, pleasant or unpleasant?
- Do you have any prior experience with this method? If so, can you set aside that past experience and have a fresh look at it?
- Take a few moments to contemplate this method and consider if you'd like to try it now or set it aside for now and come back to it later?

Mirror Work

This may be a new one for you if you haven't done some personal development work. It's not as widely used as some of the other techniques but it is powerful. It's a method used in various forms and formats by psychologists, course leaders, healers, and others. If you've heard of the late Louise Hay, you'll find that she created an entire course on Mirror Work, alone. If you're interested, please seek it out on her website, LouiseHay.com.

Mirror work, essentially, entails looking into a mirror, focusing on your eyes and allowing yourself to let go of anything else from your attention. Allow yourself to really look into your own eyes, trying to identify the You that lies within.

The idea here is to get in touch with that inner part of you, perhaps the inner child, the wounded one who has been seeking your attention all your life. The part of you that you had to set aside at one point because the wound was too great and beyond your ability to heal when it happened. But, you had to go on. You had to pick up and carry on in the world of people and, so, part of you was left behind.

You look in the mirror and see what words come to mind, what question might be looming there, what unanswered need. From there, you give yourself permission to provide that unanswered need, to answer that question, to give the love and attention that you weren't able to or aware of needing at the time.

Now, as a responsible, powerful, caring, nurturing adult, you can give that part of yourself the care and attention it needs.

Mirror work is a daily practice. Repeating phrases to yourself in the mirror, either phrases that you've uncovered as you go or simply, *I love you.* Your phrase must be said with true emotion, with true love and you must allow your love to flow freely. Doing so creates a sense of relief and, as you allow yourself to become comfortable with it, you'll experience a sense of rightness and confidence, a sense of power and assurance and, of course, love.

There's so much depth in this work and it's very powerful. When I first heard of it at a church I attended, I followed the instructions and wrote out the phrase I love you on 3" x 5" index cards. Those cards were taped up on every mirror in my house and car. I did my damnedest to look in the mirror every day and tell myself *I love you.*

I admit that I felt like a fraud, though. This was in the early 90's and life was go-go-go at the time. Two kids, a career at a fortune 100 company working 10+ hours a day, an ex-husband, and a burning desire to feel loved that I tried to fill in a revolving door of monogamous relationships that didn't work. You can't give what you don't have. I didn't really know how to love at the time. I kept those cards, or something similar like a sticky-note, on my mirrors and fridge and front door for years. The next time I came across this exercise was during an emotion-based personal development course in Florida called The Loving Course or TLC.

Our course instructor, Rita, worked with me, holding a large oval mirror in her lap while I sat across from her, gazing into it. We were supported by a number of other attendees whose sole purpose was to give moral support to the person doing the emotionally charged work. I was very grateful to have those people there supporting me.

One of the biggest beliefs I had to tackle was the belief that I was unlovable, that no one would want to be with me if they knew who I truly was, and that everyone would leave me eventually. I would be ridiculed and laughed at and eventually be left all alone. These beliefs, I came to find out through the mirror work, are an aspect of shame.

I came to see a part of me that I'd left behind when I was a little girl. A part of me who still yearned for love and approval. From that exercise, I set up a daily ritual that had me singing a phrase from a song each morning while I gazed into my own eyes. I can definitely say that it felt strange and weird at first and was difficult to get used to. I started and stopped at first but eventually realized that I always felt better after I'd done it and my day always went more smoothly.

I don't sing to myself every day anymore but I do look at myself in the mirror and tell myself *I love you*. I still have a note on my mirror that says, *I love you,* and I still feel better when I take the time to look into my own eyes and acknowledge *me*.

So, if you take this one on, know that you have the ability to do some truly deep and important work for yourself. You have an opportunity to access some deeply hidden sources of fear, shame, anger, and sadness and give yourself some much-needed love to heal.

Questions to ask yourself:

- When you think of this method, do you have any physical reaction, pleasant or unpleasant?
- Do you have any prior experience with this method? If so, can you set aside that past experience and have a fresh look at it?
- Take a few moments to contemplate this method and consider if you'd like to try it now or set it aside for now and come back to it later?

Ho'oponopono

This is a Hawaiian method for instilling healing based on love and forgiveness that a friend introduced to me many years ago. I've used this to help diffuse tumultuous situations with family and friends. I'm not an expert and I have no empirical evidence that it works but I do know that it helped reduce the amount of anxiety I experienced. I'm talking about divorce, custody battles, friendships threatened by breakups and mistrust. Things of this nature.

The process, as I understand it and practiced it, consists of holding the object of your healing and forgiveness in your mind, a picture is helpful if you have one. Do your best to feel the energy of your heart and intend for it to expand. At the same time, focus on the other person(s), individually, and repeat the phrase (as if it's a mantra), *I'm sorry. Please, forgive me. I love you.*

Maintain your focus and the mantra with your heart energy expanded until you experience a release or a relaxing of the tension. Repeat the process with everyone involved. Do this on a daily basis until there's a shift in the circumstances. It's said that the power of this exercise can drastically change the demeanor and behavior of those involved. You'll have to see for yourself as the only way I can explain it is through the power of love and intention.

Questions to ask yourself:
- When you think of this method, do you have any physical reaction, pleasant or unpleasant?

- Do you have any prior experience with this method? If so, can you set aside that past experience and have a fresh look at it?
- Take a few moments to contemplate this method and consider if you'd like to try it now or set it aside for now and come back to it later?

Forgiveness Writing

This is a writing exercise that takes the power of forgiveness and amplifies it. The premise is that by forgiving, you set yourself free. You're not saying that what they did or what happened is right. You're not condoning behavior that's hurtful or hateful.

But, holding onto grievances is self-destructive. It imprisons you. It poisons you. It creates a continued tie to that person and the event that upset you. When you forgive, you give yourself a gift. You're saying that you're not going to carry around the weight of all that baggage and let it continue to poison your present moment with the past.

The process:

Write out a list of the people you're still holding some kind of grievance against. Someone you blame for an event in your life or someone who angered you, hurt you or wounded you in some way. Then write the line below as many times as you need to, 10, 20, 50, whatever it takes until you feel a release.

You may need to set a number for each one and then continue the following day(s) until you can think about that person(s) without the usual accompanying discomfort or upset.

I forgive you, (fill in their name) and I set myself free unless I choose to use you to imprison myself again.

Remember, forgiveness isn't about letting anyone off the hook. It's about freeing yourself from the torment of holding onto the past.

Questions to ask yourself:

- When you think of this method, do you have any physical reaction, pleasant or unpleasant?
- Do you have any prior experience with this method? If so, can you set aside that past experience and have a fresh look at it?
- Take a few moments to contemplate this method and consider if you'd like to try it now or set it aside for now and come back to it later?

Self-Care

Make Your Self Important or Nurture Your Seedlings or Provide Sunshine and Rain to Your New Inner Garden

Taking care of your Self is vitally important. It's the foundation for making your life work. It's the foundation for making sure you can be there for your loved ones. When you make your Self-important, you send a message throughout your body, mind, and soul that you matter. You also send a message to everyone in your life that you are important, that you have boundaries, and that' you're going to do whatever it takes to make sure you meet your inner needs.

This creates a different relationship with people. Some people will love this change you're making and others will squawk that you're being selfish. They squawk because you've probably always done for them at your own expense.

Sacrificing something that's important to you because they had something they wanted from you. Every time you did this, you gave away a piece of you, you chipped away at your sense of self-esteem, self-confidence, and self-worth.

After a while, you don't have much left to give. You grow resentful, tired, drained, empty, angry, frustrated, bitter, fragile, and are left with nothing but the shell of who you really are.

If you've been on an airplane, you know that they tell you to secure your air mask before you try to help anyone else. The same holds true for your broader life. If you don't give yourself the care, nurturing and importance in your own life, you really don't have anything to offer anyone else.

Below is a list of various items that I consider important elements of self-care. You don't need to do all of them, of course, but choose several and try them out.

Try something new and see how it feels, experiment, have fun and, above all, take good care of yourself.

- **Sleep** – Co-#1 most important self-care item
- **Hydration** – Co-#1 single most important self-care item (the symptoms are so vast that I can't list them all here). I have 1 oz. water for every 2 lbs. of my body weight and I always feel better when I meet this requirement.
- **Nutrition** – Co-#1 – eat good, clean, wholesome, from-scratch food and eliminate the processed items, carbs and highly starchy foods that fill you full of extra chemicals and non-nutrients that add more stress
- Spend time in nature – the woods, the beach, a country field (this resets your natural rhythms and cycles)
- Exercise/movement – perform some type of movement every day, walking is an essential. Next, add in movement that helps you slim, align, build strength and perform at your optimum like Pilates, Yoga, Tai Chi, sprints, Paleo workouts, CrossFit, or a sport that requires full-body motion

- Bath time – water is both invigorating and relaxing. Indulge with a glass of wine or another refreshment, some candles, soft music, something to read and keep that door shut and locked. For some, this is the only time you get alone
- Massage – there is a healing power in therapeutic touch
- Mani/Pedi – for the most part women may choose this but it's just as healing for men
- Pets – cuddling and loving on them decreases stress
- Relaxing with friends and loved ones
- Getting creative: painting, drawing, pottery, woodwork, mechanics, welding, forging, gardening, etc.
- A hobby that gets you out of the house >/ once a week
- Delegate – ask for help, don't "do" everything, especially in your home if you live with others. Everyone should have a set of tasks they're responsible for.
- Say "NO" and mean it – It's a classic but it bears stating here. If someone asks you to do something and you feel a pull in your gut, that's a sign to say no.

☺

Part 4

Creating Your Plan

*If you want something new, you have to
stop doing something old. – Peter Drucker*

There are as many ways to arrange your schedule
and daily routine as there are people. This
section is about setting yourself up to win,
setting goals that you can work with, goals that
stimulate you to carry on, with small milestones that
you can celebrate and timelines that bring you ease.

When you're creating your plan, try to set aside your
past experiences with any of the methods and approach
it with a fresh perspective. I know that's not as easy as
it sounds but putting everything together in a cohesive
plan might make a difference in the way that works for
you.

In this section, I've listed what I usually do on a daily
basis. I'm not a stickler on it and if I miss something, I
don't beat myself up for it but do what I can to make
sure I'm set to have a fantastic day.

If you don't have any real ritual in the morning except rolling out of bed, grabbing a coffee and running out the door, don't try to load everything on yourself at once. Be gentle and Let it be Easy. Take on one or two things at a time, incorporating them a week at a time until you've found the perfect combination for you. Be flexible. There's no right or wrong way to do this.

Identifying and Claiming Your Sacred Space

You may not realize it yet, but you need your own sacred space. Having a place you can go that you call your own, where you can reclaim what is truly unique about you, recharge, align, meditate, be creative or whatever it is you've discovered you need to refill You, is imperative. You need a space that they can call your own, where you feel safe, secure, and secluded. Where you can completely let go of the outside world.

For some, this is a separate room with objects that have been collected, comfortable seating, appealing colors and materials, soft lighting and airflow. For others, their sacred space may be anywhere they can play their guitar with abandon, a path through a natural setting, the kitchen, the bathtub, the piano, in front of the easel, on the dancefloor or any such setting where relaxation, creativity, and creation take place.

You may already know what your sacred space is. If so, make sure you've staked a claim on it and set a boundary with anyone else who may be in your environment so it's known that this space is solely for your use when you need to recharge. Make sure you are firm about not being disturbed while you're using your space if you need privacy. For most, any type of meditation requires quiet so be sure to make this known.

If you live with others, especially a spouse and children, make sure they know you love them and that this is an important time for you. This sets an example for self-care that goes far beyond any words in instilling self-esteem and confidence in your children. You may get opposition but be firm in setting your boundary.

Eventually, it will become part of the norm in your household and others may even follow suit, beginning to take good care of themselves and feeling better because of the example you set. (I'm not saying your kids will come out and tell you this in the moment but they may eventually.)

Daily Rituals

Start and End Your Day with Mindful Purpose
You already have many daily routines. You're probably not even aware of them because they're so habitual. You wake up every morning, get out of bed, have breakfast, exercise, brush your teeth, shower, get dressed, take the dog out, get the kids ready, drive to work, run errands, and on and on.

So what we're really talking about here is making your daily routines more purposeful, creating mindfulness and alignment with your new outlook and way of life. You're going to build in some segments that take your inner needs into consideration and that leads to a richer, fuller, more successful

Morning Rituals – 30 - 60 Minutes

What you do first thing in the morning sets the tone for the rest of your day. It's essential that you set yourself up purposefully for optimum aliveness and joy.

- Start when you first realize you're awake and focus on something that makes you feel good. If worrisome thoughts try to crowd in (perhaps because they haven't been addressed properly during the day by being written down and scheduled to be taken care of), set them aside and continue to look for thoughts that make you feel good. This doesn't have to be a long process, just a few minutes is sufficient, to begin with, unless you choose this time to do your morning meditation.

- Next, stretch and activate every part of your body, from your toes, feet, and ankles to your hands and wrists to your face, head, and neck. Move, tense and relax, and stretch each part to wake it up before you put a toe out of bed

- If you do oil pulling as part of your oral hygiene ritual do that now along with the rest of your oral hygiene ritual

- Drink at least ½ liter of clean, filtered, pH balanced water immediately, or the cleanest water you can find. Your body has been without for 7-8 hours or more and it needs a boost. It worked hard during that time, repairs, maintenance and etc. Give it a hand by giving it some hydration.

- Move your body in some way. Walk, strength training, aerobics, etc. There are many benefits to doing your exercise first thing in the morning. You set your body up for increased fat burning throughout the day; you feel more energized throughout the day; you get it out of the way so you don't have anything co-opting your afternoon or evening workout plans. (Drink another ½ liter of water for every ½ hour of exercise you perform to replace what you sweat out.)

- Eat a healthy, nutritious, clean breakfast. I have a green protein shake every morning and blend it so it's easy to drink. I use a NutriBullet™ but you can use whatever you have on hand. It's easy to make, especially when I prep the container with everything I need the night before. I add greens (my favorite combo is spinach, cilantro, and parsley), ¼ inch of fresh ginger – skin and all, spices for all their amazing qualities as well as flavor (Ceylon cinnamon, ginger, turmeric, cayenne pepper), unsweetened protein powder (the spices and greens add the flavor). I also have fresh garlic separately.

- Meditate for 15 – 20 minutes using whatever method works best for you. If you've never meditated before, now is the time to start. It's the practice of clearing your mind and managing your thoughts so they don't run amuck on you during the day. The main thing to remember is to breath steadily with an in-breath of 3 or 4 and an out-breath that is longer (i.e. in for 3 counts, out for 5 counts). You can download a guided meditation on my website, giacilento.com/meditation

- Check your bedside journal for any items you need to address that came up for you the night before. Prioritize in a way that relieves stress about any particular item *and* has you moving forward in the important areas. It's easy to get bogged down with

- Shower and get ready for the rest of your day. After you've washed, rinse and end your shower with a couple minutes of cold water. Turn your water cold enough to make a difference. Rinse your hair and face, then the rest of your body and end with it on your neck and back. I find that it closes my pores and helps relax my back. You'll feel refreshed and alive when you've finished.

Evening Rituals – 20 - 30 minutes

Having a ritual at the end of your day helps you sleep peacefully and clears the slate so you can wake up with control over your thoughts.

- Begin to get ready for bed at least 30 minutes before you actually want to fall asleep
- Take care of your oral hygiene, if you don't use oil pulling, I suggest looking it up and incorporating it into your routine, also use an organic, non-toxic toothpaste
- Keep a journal beside your bed and use it each evening to recap and clear your day from your mind. Write down what you're grateful for that day, what wins you experienced, what you'd like to do differently in the future and anything that may still be on your mind that was left undone

- Make sure your environment is quiet and serene
- Make sure your bed is comfortable, clean and your pillow is supportive
- Darken your room
- Lie down and begin to breathe rhythmically as you would when you meditate with a steady in breath for 3 counts and out-breath for 5 counts.
- Bring your attention from anything else in your life and focus on you and where you are. Feel the pillow beneath your head, the sheets against your skin, the mattress supporting your body and the breath entering and leaving you.
- Maintain your focus on your breathing until you fall asleep, usually, you'll turn to your most comfortable position naturally

Longer Rituals

Weekly

On a weekly basis, set aside time for a longer, deeper recharge, totally unplugged. No news, no internet, no phone. This may take some doing, especially if you're married (with children or without). If you're single, it may be somewhat easier, depending on the number of responsibilities you have. One day would be wonderful but if you can't-do a whole day, try for a block of eight hours, six hours at a minimum.

Use this time to explore and indulge in everything you enjoy that stimulates your creativity, relaxes your mind, and relaxes your body. For example, walking along the beach, visiting museums, art galleries, painting or some other form of creativity, going to the spa for a massage or some other sort of physical pamperings like a facial, mani/pedi and etc. Really think about the things you enjoy doing that you don't often allow yourself to do.

This is the time you would set aside to do those things on purpose and mindfully, allowing yourself to fill with gratitude and acknowledging yourself (and your loved ones, if suitable) for giving yourself this gift.

Monthly

Your monthly ritual is an expanded version of your weekly one. Arrange to have 3-4 days away from everything, optimally, 1-2 days if that's not possible. Over time, you'll find that this refresh and rejuvenation time adds so much value to your life that you'll do whatever you need do to have it happen and eventually you'll find an easy flow happening that allows you to take the time away that you need.

Annually

An annual getaway is imperative; especially if you've found that you haven't quite yet accomplished giving yourself the monthly and weekly time you need. Get entirely away and unplugged. These can be family times together, too, when you can unplug and unwind together but make sure you still give yourself alone time

☺
Conclusion

Managing stress is a life-long process. You will always have stress in your life and learning to manage it properly will not only bring you joy but will lead to a healthier, happier life. Living your life with your focus on unconditional joy gives you the ability to choose your outlook moment by moment and, therefore, choose your outcome.

You can go as deep as you want with any of the exercises. Remember to be easy on yourself and set a pace that allows you to flow with whatever comes up. If you feel overwhelmed at any time, take a break. This isn't a race. There's no need to hurry or rush yourself.

As you begin to shift your habits to those gratitude, love, and appreciation and start to see the world through unconditional joy you'll find it easier and easier to maintain. Start slowly, adding one or two new routines a week until you've built an ideal lifestyle for yourself.

What happens next is entirely up to you. When you have a powerful place to stand within and you've created a method to be in the world and still have dominion over Self, you open up opportunities and possibilities that didn't exist before.

When you get to that place, you'll know you've anchored in a new way of being. You'll start to see things differently. You'll notice when someone is yelling or angry that they're actually in a conflict with themselves. You'll notice that someone who's withdrawn and quiet might actually need a friendly smile or a word of encouragement.

You'll start to see people and events and interactions differently. You'll see them more as what they really are, something having to do with that person's inner environment running amuck, rather than taking them personally and thinking you need to defend or protect or run.

You'll have true freedom and true strength. You'll know it and you'll love every moment of it.

Thank you for taking on this journey. I firmly believe that when there are enough people who own their inner world and stand in place of unconditional joy as their inner strength, we'll reach a tipping point and the world as we currently know it will shift.

☺
Resources and Recommended Reading

You Can Heal Your Life – Louise Hay
The Bible
A Course in Miracles – Foundation for Inner Peace
The Seven Spiritual Laws of Success – Deepak Chopra
Creating Affluence – Deepak Chopra
Living with Joy – Sanaya Roman
E^2, E^3, and Thank & Grow Rich – Pam Grout
Johnathan Livingston Seagull – Richard Bach
Body Mind Mastery – Dan Millman
A Return to Love – Marianne Williamson
The New Earth – Eckhart Tolle
The Four Agreements – Don Miguel Ruiz
Conversations with God (Book 1) – Neale Donald Walsh
The Prophet – Khalil Gibran
Eat, Pray, Love – Elizabeth Gilbert
Your Body Believes Every Word You Say, – Barbara Hoberman Levine
Think and Grow Rich – Napoleon Hill
The TLC Course, Florida – Rita Homrich, http://thelivingcourse.org/
Summit Trainings
The Landmark Courses

How to Development Self-Confidence and Influence People by Public Speaking – Dale Carnegie

The Science of Getting Rich – Wallace D. Wattles

Power vs. Force – David R. Hawkins, M.D.

The Prayer of St. Francis – James Twyman

One Planet United - Jack Bloomfield

Healing and the Mind – Bill Moyers

Source Movement – Jo Englesson

The Vortex – Esther and Jerry Hicks – The Teachings of Abraham

☺

Acknowledgements

For some reason, this one stumped me at first and I didn't know where to start.

There are so many people who have added love, guidance, and inspiration to my life. I could write volumes about each one and still not convey the depth of my gratitude for those who poured themselves out in support or who set an example.

The only solution that makes sense is a list in random order. Otherwise, this book would never end and the printing cost, not to mention the weight, would be prohibitive.

Please accept my deepest gratitude Rita Homrich, Francine Rahe, Barry Warren, Ken and Kathy Cushman, Bennet Bramson, Naomi Dunford, Tara Marino, the late Beth Seidle, the late David Persichini, the late Joe Cavanaugh, Judith Rich, Kathy Benson, Steffie Loveless, Claudia Rauch, Sarah Seidle, Monica Ogando, Maida Wilson, Verna Edington,

A big shout out to everyone at Mad Hatter Publishing, Inc. who helped make this work possible.

Thank you to my sister, Abby, and her husband, Rob, for always being there when I need them and always being ready with a great meal, a wonderful glass of wine and *interesting* conversation.

To all my siblings, Adie, Penny, Abby, Ben, Viv, Jules and Raffy and my late sister, Naomi, for giving me a lifetime of love, excitement, and togetherness that helped me make it through our tumultuous childhood.

A big thank you to my friends who opened their hearts to me and supply me with love, and a sense of belonging, and community, especially Vivian, Liberty, Susan, and Jeanne.

I wouldn't be where I am without the love and support of my mother, Mavis Salus. I love you, Mom. Thank you to my father, Dr. Raphael Cilento, and my step-father, Howard Salus, for many reasons.

Keeping me going with love and chocolate, my wife, Wendy.

Providing inspiration and a drive to always move forward, my children, Naomi, and Sean and Andrea, and my grandchildren, Micah and Diana.

And, finally, an ever-expanding level of love, appreciation, and gratitude to God or Source/All-That-Is/Universe (a name can be so limiting).

☺

About the Author

Giovanna "Gia" Cilento (1961 -) was born in London, England, and emigrated to the United States at three months old. Her family moved about the United States, often spending time back in her parents' home country, Australia. By the time she was ten years old, she'd moved approximately 20 times and traveled extensively. The people she met along the way and the experiences she gained sparked her imagination and created a love for the written word that would shape her life.

Today, Ms. Cilento is an award-winning writer, noted publisher, life-coach, and communications expert. Her career in publishing spans nearly 30 years. She has extensive experience in print and digital media, writing, editing, coaching, as well as leading and managing projects and creative teams.

Gia first joined the publishing world as a part-time typesetter in the mid-80's and quickly fell in love. She'd always loved books, reading (she spent hours in libraries), and writing and the publishing industry brought a welcome outlet for her passions.

Moving through various positions at the newspaper, she soon became the Production Director and computerized the production of the small local entertainment paper, one of the first to do so in the state of Florida and found a love for technology along the way.

When she first learned of the internet in the mid-90's, the full potential it offered hadn't yet been explored. Throughout the ensuing years, she researched ways to combine her love of publishing with internet technology and the burgeoning online publishing industry.

Today, she runs a growing publishing company, Mad Hatter Publishing, Inc., partnering with talented and passionate writers and also writes her own books that aim to help people create a fantastic life.

With a passion for words and creating, she spends her spare time (when she stumbles upon it) staring at blank pages, imagining the joy of filling them up with her thoughts and imaginings.

Gia lives in Southeast Michigan with her wife, two dogs, and a cat.

Coming this fall by Mad Hatter Publishing, Inc.

From our Motor City Press Imprint
Elephant   Play   by   David   Ryals
DavidRyals.com
A novel that takes us on a journey into madness
entwined with a glimpse into the gruesome and brutal
ivory trade. An expressive work inspired by absurdity
and satirized through vibrant caricature. Molded from
the genius of the likes of F. Scott Fitzgerald, Vladimir
Nabokov and Ralph Ellison (among others), Mr. Ryals
emerges as his generation's most inspired novelist.
The strongest impression *Elephant Play* leaves on its
'silent readers' is that Ryals is not only a skilled
psychological observer but also a strident moralist. His
diabolic narrator is driven by a ghastly sense of
helpless futility, born in the poorest part of America,
but also a compulsive criminality that keeps his chance
at fame in sight. It is a measure of the authors' power
that he makes us live through that hideous dream and
unlike his narrator, emerge from it illuminated. Or,
bewildered. Or, diabolically amused.

From our Minerva Press imprint
*Narcissistic Personality Disorder – No Band-Aid for a
Wounded Soul* by Sara Teller
SaraTeller.com
Ms. Teller brings to bear her life experience combined
with her intellectual and academic studies and presents
a thorough reference book addressing the differences
between   healthy   narcissism   and   Narcissistic

Personality Disorder (NPD). Three distinct and separate sections focus on:

- Narcissism as an inherent humanistic trait versus pathological narcissism
- Victimization and the healing process
- Therapeutic intervention

Dark of Night by AM Paoletti
AMPaoletti.com
A gritty thriller/romance based in Detroit, MI. A terrorist is planning something big in Detroit just in time for the President's visit. Antonia "Toni" Andiamo discovers it's the same man who captured and tortured her in Afghanistan, the same man who ordered her family killed. She's on a mission of revenge. Dealing with the Federal Task Force, FBI, an "unofficial" CIA agent, and an attractive Special Agent in Charge she chases her enemy, knowing that time is running out.

From our Expansion Press Imprint
Billy of Flawn by Sammy Ogg
MadHatterPublishingInc.com
Inspired the by the death of his young son in 1976, Sammy Ogg - a child actor in the 50's and 60's - takes us on a fantastic journey with Billy as he finds himself in Flawn, a kingdom in another dimension for children after he's struck by a car. His guardian angels, Cypress and Hollyb, tell him that Elohim has a plan to help all the children of Flawn and has called Billy to leave earth early to carry it out. You'll discover Billy's purpose and

follow him as he fulfills Elohim's request and takes all the children of Flawn with him.

From the Brink of Suicide – How an 11th-Hour Revelation Made Her Put the Gun Down by Adrian
MadHatterPublishingInc.com

This is a true story of neglect, abuse, and a lifetime of depression leading to one fateful night when suicide seemed like the only option. Sexually assaulted by an uncle at a very young age, she was ignored and then sent away when she tried to find help from her parents and other adults. The scars left behind tore through her life leaving her teetering from depression to mania. Doctors and medication were of no help. One night, with a gun in her hand, she came face to face with her inner demon and found that she had the power to banish him. That night, she wrote the main part of this short book, "In Search of the Emerald City".

Choosing to go only by "Adrian" to protect her children, we learn about her early life and the trauma that caused her so much pain. Her message: depression is only a fierce demon until you choose to chase it down and confront it. Once you find your demon, you have the power to banish him for good. There's no promises made, no panacea, but her life continues as an example to others who struggle with depression and thoughts of suicide.

If you've ever been touched by suicide, this book will shed some light. If you've ever contemplated suicide, this book will be very familiar.

www.ingramcontent.com/pod-product-compliance
Lightning Source LLC
Chambersburg PA
CBHW031043110426
42740CB00048B/978